RELENTLESS

MY LIFE IN HOCKEY AND
THE POWER OF PERSEVERANCE

BRYAN BERARD

with JIM LANG

PUBLISHED BY SIMON & SCHUSTER

NEW YORK   LONDON   TORONTO   SYDNEY   NEW DELHI

SIMON &
SCHUSTER
CANADA

Simon & Schuster Canada
A Division of Simon & Schuster, Inc.
166 King Street East, Suite 300
Toronto, Ontario M5A 1J3

This Simon & Schuster Canada edition October 2019

SIMON & SCHUSTER CANADA and colophon are trademarks of Simon & Schuster, Inc.

For information about special discounts for bulk purchases, please contact
Simon & Schuster Special Sales at 1-800-268-3216 or CustomerService@simonandschuster.ca.

Manufactured in Canada

1   3   5   7   9   10   8   6   4   2

Library and Archives Canada Cataloguing in Publication

Title: Relentless : my life in hockey and the power of
perseverance / by Bryan Berard with Jim Lang.
Names: Berard, Bryan, 1977- author. | Lang, Jim, 1965- author.
Identifiers: Canadiana (print) 20190103213 | Canadiana (ebook) 20190102926
| ISBN 9781982130268 (hardcover) | ISBN 9781982130299 (ebook)
Subjects: LCSH: Berard, Bryan, 1977- | LCSH: Hockey players—
United States—Biography. | LCGFT: Autobiographies.
Classification: LCC GV848.5.B47 A3 2019 | DDC 796.962092—dc23

ISBN 978-1-9821-3026-8
ISBN 978-1-9821-3029-9 (ebook)

To my parents

CONTENTS

PROLOGUE

LAY IN THE HOSPITAL BED, THE GAUZE STRETCHED TIGHT AROUND MY HEAD TO hold the bandages in place over my right eye. A stack of machines blinked and beeped beside me, and I heard the rumble of conversation in the hallway outside my room.

I looked toward the window, where my mom was sitting quietly in a chair.

"How are you feeling?" she asked.

A flurry of responses raced through my brain. *Worried. Angry. Scared. Confused.* "Exhausted," I said finally. I tried to think back to what had happened a few nights before in Ottawa. One moment, I'd been patrolling the front of the net, trying to clear the puck out of our zone. The next, I was lying, kicking and screaming, in a pool of my own blood.

"The doctors will be back soon to talk about how the surgery went," my mom said.

I nodded. I knew what they were going to say, and what it meant for me. "My career is over," I said. "I'm never going to play in the NHL again."

My mom turned to me, a stern look on her face. "'Never' does not exist in our family's vocabulary."

I was stunned. My mom could sense my surprise, and she continued, "Anything is possible. It might not be easy—it will take a lot of hard work. But if you want to play in the NHL again, that's what you'll do."

One year, six months, and twenty-six days later—five hundred and seventy-five days after my injury—my mom's words came true. It was October 7, 2001, and that night, I was going to lace up my skates for my first home game with the New York Rangers.

I woke up that morning in my apartment on the Upper West Side of Manhattan and looked across the city skyline outside my window. I thought I'd be nervous, but I was too excited to feel the nerves. I was back.

I headed to the subway, stopping along the way for one of my few game-day routines: having a Krispy Kreme donut on the way to the morning skate. I emerged from the subway after a few stops, and when I got up to the street, I saw Madison Square Garden in front of me. As a member of the New York Islanders, I had played the Rangers at MSG many times. The Rangers had been our mortal enemy. It was ironic, then, that I was making my comeback to the league as a member of the team that I was taught to hate. It had been over a month since my first day at training camp with the Rangers, but walking through the doors of MSG each day still gave me goose bumps.

Damn, this feels good, I thought.

I gave Brian Leetch a wave as we headed to the dressing room. When we got there, Mark Messier was taping his stick in his stall.

"How are you doing today, B?" Leetch asked.

"Never felt better, Leetchie," I said with a grin.

I'd started training camp a few weeks back feeling less than my usual self, like I was half a step slow or the puck wouldn't quite settle down for me. Each day, though, I felt a little stronger and a little faster—playing alongside the many talented veterans on the Rangers that year helped me get my timing back in a hurry. Leetch and Messier, along with all the other guys on the team, had been an incredible support along the way, making sure I felt like I belonged and that I could do this.

After our pregame skate, I headed back to my apartment for a nap. A few hours later, I was back on the subway, heading to the rink for the game (this time, without a donut).

I thought that the jitters might finally set in as the puck drop approached, but as I got dressed for the game, my body was humming from nerves and excitement. Nobody said anything special to me in the dressing room before the game, though. It was business as usual. This was just another game, and I was just another player on the team.

I did finally feel a chill go down my spine as the lights dimmed for the national anthem. Our game that night against the Buffalo Sabres was less than a month after 9/11, and the Rangers held a big pregame ceremony to honor the New York firefighters and police officers who had saved lives—many of them losing their own in the process—during the disaster. The city was still hurting, and as the anthem played, I felt a stirring in my chest and a deep gratitude for their courage. Any struggles I might have had along the way paled in comparison to what was happening in New York City at the time.

When I jumped over the boards for my first shift, I could feel the adrenaline rushing through my blood. It felt amazing. The roar of the crowd filled my ears, and each time I felt my edges dig into the ice, I felt the need to go faster, skate harder, and dig deeper.

I knew my mom was going to be a nervous wreck watching the game. But she had no reason to be nervous. Not only were my teammates looking out for me, so were opposing players.

Before each face-off, guys would skate up to me and tap my shin pads, saying "Nice to see you back." Every single time, I would smile sheepishly and thank them for the kind words. They extended the same respect during play, too. When veteran forwards chased me in the corner, they would give me a heads-up and tell me what side they were on. Instead of running me through the boards, they would warn me where they were coming from, to give me a chance to make a play. They weren't taking it easy, but I appreciated the courtesy.

It wasn't all smooth, though—as enthusiastic as I was, I was still learning how to see the game differently. I had problems when two forwards were chasing me down in the corner. When I picked the puck up and went to spin out, I could tell where the first guy was, but I struggled picking up the second guy. Every time I made a mistake, though, I refused to let it get to me. *Next time, don't rely on your peripherals,* I thought as I caught my breath on the bench. *You need to learn to look at the game differently.*

Halfway through the game, I was sitting on the bench waiting for my next shift and some of the frustration caught up to me.

"Between this stupid visor and my nose, there's too much getting in the way," I grumbled. "I've got no peripheral."

Leetch looked at me and said, "Why don't you just have someone shave your nose down a little bit, B? That will help your other eye." I immediately started laughing like crazy, along with the other guys on the bench. Leetch was one of the quietest guys I had ever played with, and he never said much during a game, so none of us could believe he'd cracked a joke.

Brian's comment put things in perspective, and I turned my focus back to the game. This was my new normal, and I had to find a way to make it work.

Our coach, Ron Low, kept calling my name that night, and I kept hopping over the boards. I was so excited all game that I even blocked a couple of shots. My mom's heart probably skipped a beat when she saw me slide to the ice to block each one.

I was grateful for the Rangers giving me the opportunity to come back. I was slotted as the fifth or sixth defenseman for the year, but I didn't care because I was back in the NHL. Every night I stepped on the ice that year felt like a gift on Christmas morning.

I knew some people weren't convinced that I could play at the NHL level with one eye. I would never be able to play the same way I had before my injury. But at least I could play. When you want something badly enough, you find a way.

There was still a long road ahead. I had wanted to play in the NHL my entire life, and I would have to earn my place every step of the way. But I knew I wouldn't stop.

Never?

I don't think so. Not in my family.

1

WOONSOCKET ROCKET

I AM PROUD TO SAY THAT I WAS BORN AND RAISED IN WOONSOCKET, RHODE Island. When I was growing up, Woonsocket was a textile town by day and a hockey town by night. During the week, most of the town's seventy to eighty thousand people worked in and around the town's mills. On the evenings and weekends, though, life revolved around the hockey rink. Woonsocket had a lot of people of French Canadian descent, so there was a healthy rivalry between the Montreal Canadiens fans and those who cheered for the closer-to-home Boston Bruins.

Even when I was young, though, I had to be different from everyone else, so I decided that I would be a fan of the Pittsburgh Penguins. Mario Lemieux was my favorite player. Every time I practiced my wrist shot in the basement or played a game of street hockey, I'd pretend I was Lemieux about to score the Stanley Cup–winning goal.

I was born on March 5, 1977, the oldest of my mom and dad's

kids. My dad, Wally, had been married before he met my mom, Pam, so I had an older half brother, Dave, and a half sister, Linda, and we all grew up together. In the years after I was born, I was followed by my younger brother, Greg, my sister, Bethany, and my youngest sibling, Bruce.

We lived on a cul-de-sac in East Woonsocket, in a raised-ranch bungalow that my dad built with his friends. All those bodies under one roof made for a crowded home, but we never minded. We were a tight-knit family, and the door was always open to family, friends, and neighbors. It seemed our house was the central hangout for everyone in the neighborhood, whether it was kids coming over to play street hockey in our driveway—we regularly had six to eight guys for our games—or adults looking for my dad's advice on a car issue. We also had a pool, so when the weather was nice, our house became the daily center of activity for all of my and my siblings' friends.

My dad was a mechanic and he owned his own garage—Broad Street Garage—on (you guessed it) Broad Street in Woonsocket. As he got older, though, he realized he needed a job with benefits and a pension, so he took a job as the head of the Smithfield School facilities. Essentially, he was the building superintendent. Day to day, that meant he was in charge of taking care of the school, making sure that it was clean and that nothing was broken. But during the winter, he had real power—on the really snowy days, he was the one who headed to the school early in the morning and decided whether it would be a snow day. On those mornings, my siblings and I would anxiously wait at the door for my dad to return, hoping that he'd set us free for the day.

We spent a lot of time in my dad's shop when I was younger. My siblings didn't mind it, but I did. I liked hanging out with my dad—I just hated getting my hands dirty. I was constantly trying to sweep the floor or clean the counters to get rid of some of the grime. Every time I finished my job, my dad laughed as I raced to the sink to wash my hands.

One time, my younger brother Bruce and I were in the garage helping out my dad.

"Guys, bring me some axle grease for this car," my dad called out from across the room.

I walked up to the can of grease and poked around for a clean container to pour some of the grease into. Before I could find one, Bruce marched over, grabbed a handful of the grease out of the can, and brought it over to my dad. I was horrified, but as I watched Bruce wiping his hand on a dirty cloth, I realized that if I was the sort of person who refused to get his hands dirty, it meant other people would have to do my work for me. That wasn't something I wanted—in our family, everyone was expected to pitch in—so I promised myself that from then on, I wouldn't let it happen again.

I was more help around the house. My mom oversaw the finance and administration of my dad's garage, but she also ran the show at home. And she ran a tight ship. Each of us kids had certain chores we were delegated. I was in charge of mowing the lawn, and I enjoyed it. It got me out of the house and I liked the physical exertion. But even better, my mom also liked to mow the lawn—she saw it as her exercise—so she would often take over for me. I wasn't about to complain. The less time I spent mowing the lawn, the more I could spend playing sports.

Sports ruled my life when I was younger. All I wanted was to be on the baseball diamond or the field playing one game or another with my friends.

My best friend growing up was Brian Boucher. Years later, Brian would make it to the NHL as a star goalie. But when we met, we were just a couple of six-year-old kids who loved sports. We both had big families—Brian's family was one of those Woonsocket clans with French Canadian heritage, so they spoke French most the time at home—and siblings around the same age, so it was easy for us all to hang out. But for Brian and me in particular, it was sports all day, every day.

"Hey, Dumbo, what do you want to play today?" Brian would ask. "Dumbo" was my nickname growing up. I was a little chubby as a kid, and I don't think my ears have grown since I was six years old—my head grew bigger, but my ears stayed the same.

Most nights and weekends, Brian and I would play street hockey, baseball, football, Wiffle ball, you name it. Our house was close to a Little League baseball diamond, too, so we would bike over to play baseball on the field. Other days we would play tennis together in the park nearby. We even made up our own homemade triathlons through the neighborhood. We would go for a swim in the local pool, then get on our bikes and race up and down our streets, then run until we had stitches in our side. Basically, the only time that we ever went inside the house was to take a break and have something to eat.

We had other friends who played with us sometimes, but most days, it was Brian and me going head-to-head. We were the best of friends, and we were both so darn competitive that we pushed each other to be the best that we could be.

Our obsession with sports carried over into school. Brian and I both went to East Woonsocket School, where recess was sports time. Brian and I would both wear sweatpants and T-shirts to school every day so that we wouldn't be held back when we played sports at recess.

Brian and I were competitive—we fought all the time over little things, like who was first in a footrace or who was out of bounds on a play in two-hand touch. Sometimes we'd stand there arguing over who was right on a certain call.

"Come on, guys," our friends would say. "Let's just play."

"Shut up!" Brian and I would say in unison. Then we'd keep arguing, neither one of us willing to give in, even if it took the rest of recess and held up the game for everyone else. Most of the time, though, we were able to cool down and get back to just enjoying the game.

The fun didn't stop when we went back inside school after recess. Pantsing—or pulling down a guy's sweatpants—was a big thing for us. Whenever one of our buddies was talking to a girl, we would sneak up behind him and pull down his sweatpants. The poor guy would be standing there in his tighty-whitey underwear, his face red from embarrassment. We thought it was the funniest thing you could possibly do.

As much as I loved all sports, hockey had a special place in my life, and it got its grips into me when I was really young. I can remember the first hockey game I ever watched. It was a men's league game my dad was playing in. The moment I saw my dad hit the ice, I couldn't take my eyes off him. He was moving faster than I ever thought a person could move, and he made it look so easy. The sound of the skates cutting into the ice and the slap of the stick against the puck were imprinted on my young brain.

Then, halfway through the game, my dad chased a puck into the corner. He and the other guy got tangled up and they went hard into the boards. As my dad skated to the bench, my mom could tell something was wrong.

My dad was taken to the hospital in an ambulance. My mom

gathered me and my siblings, and we followed it to the emergency room. When we got there, the doctors told my dad he had a compound fracture. They set his arm and then he was fitted with a cast.

As we drove home, my mom kept mentioning to my dad how worried she was—she felt that seeing my dad get taken off the ice with a broken arm meant that I wouldn't want to play hockey. She didn't have anything to be concerned about, though. The moment we got home, I turned to my mom and said, "I love hockey! When do I get to play?"

I didn't have to wait long. Not long after my dad got hurt, I started skating. My brother Greg, who was three at the time, and I started off in the Woonsocket North Stars learn-to-skate program. The first time I got on the ice, I was given a big Jofa helmet and a chair to prop me up as I shuffled around the ice. The smile on my face stretched ear to ear.

Once we got a bit older, we graduated from just skating to playing shinny. We raced home from school each day, grabbed our skates and sticks, and then headed to the rink for the rest of the afternoon. The shinny games were welcoming to everyone, whether they were kids just learning to skate or men out for a game after work. As a young kid, it was the perfect way to learn the game. The older guys took it easy on me at first, letting me skate with the puck and shoot as hard as I wanted. But then, when I was on the bench, I'd watch closely how the older players stickhandled or circled around in the corner. I'd go through the same hand motions on the bench, waiting for my chance to get back on the ice and try out what I saw the older guys do.

Those self-taught lessons stuck with me—the rest of my life, I remained a visual learner, watching every play and game situation to teach myself to be a better player. It was no good if a coach or a teammate explained it to me in words. I learned best when I could watch a practice, a drill, or a game and use that to teach me how to be a better player.

Woonsocket had some good outdoor ice rinks, so my friends, siblings, and I were always on the ice. There were frozen ponds we could use for a casual skate, or we walked five minutes to the local high school, which often had an outdoor rink with boards and nets.

Of course, we would have loved to play at one of the indoor rinks. One of them, in particular. The holy grail of rinks in Woonsocket was the Adelard Arena at Mount Saint Charles, a local private school that was considered to be one of the best hockey academies in the United States. The rink was named after Brother Adelard, who founded the hockey program at the school. Decades earlier, Brother Adelard had paid two dollars for an old airport hangar and converted it into a rink for the school and community, which is why they named the rink after him. Our town team, the Woonsocket North Stars, played there, and as a young kid, I hoped that one day I'd get to pull on their jersey and step out onto the ice for a home game at Adelard Arena.

When I first started playing organized hockey at six years old, I was thicker than most kids at the time. I started off on defense, where I could stand up to kids coming down toward our goal. All that time spent playing shinny on the outdoor rinks had done me well. I wasn't much of a skater, but I was strong on my feet, and the other kids just bounced off me. My coaches, a pair of brothers named Jeff and John Robitaille, eventually started calling me "Rock."

"Good job out there, Rock," Jeff would call from the bench as I cleared the puck from the net.

The next year, when I was still bigger than the other kids around me, my new coach thought it would be a good idea for me to play forward. He put me on the wing, and I hated every second of it. Looking back, I could see that playing forward even for just that brief bit of time helped me to understand the offensive aspects of the game—how to drive to the net, how to position myself for a pass on a breakout, how to change up my speed on a rush to create space between me and the defenseman. Still, even though I wasn't ten years old yet, I knew one thing for sure—if I was going to play hockey, it was going to be as a defenseman or nothing else.

A few years later, I hit a growth spurt, and as I got taller and leaner, my skating improved. I was still always bigger than most of the kids around me, though. When I was eleven years old, my buddies and I went to sign up for Pop Warner football. As part of the tryout, the league weighed each of the kids. At that level, if you weighed 105 pounds or less, you played in the Cobra B league. If you weighed more than that, you played in the Cobra A league. Sure enough, all my buddies were under 105 pounds and were put in the Cobra B league. I weighed 110 pounds, though, which meant I wouldn't be allowed to play football with any of my friends.

To heck with that, I thought. I only wanted to do it to be with my friends. So I quit the league instead.

It wasn't that big a loss. I still had baseball, another game I loved. I played shortstop and pitched, and when I played Little League, some of the all-star teams I played on did pretty well. Brian played on the same team as me, and the same year that I decided not to play football, we won the Rhode Island state title. After that, we headed to Connecticut to play for regional title. If we won the tournament, we'd advance to the Little League World Series.

We had a tough tournament—we were knocked out of the round robin, and in one of our games, a line drive hit me in the face and broke my nose. Still, just playing at that level was a big deal to me and the other guys on the team. ESPN covered the tournament, and playing in front of the cameras made us feel like professionals.

Some of the kids I played hockey with went to performance camps in the summer. Not me, though. My dad thought it was important to take a break from hockey over the summer. Plus, hockey was an expensive sport, and money was getting a bit tight for our family.

My dad had started having some bad luck with his garage. Woonsocket was a tough place, and there were often break-ins at businesses around town. My dad's garage was broken into twice. The first time, they stole our dogs. We had a Rottweiler and a German shepherd. They came home with us on the weekends, but during the week, they slept at the garage to guard my dad's tools. One morning, though, my dad showed up to work and the dogs were gone. Sadly, we later learned that they'd been stolen for dog fighting.

The next break-in was worse. The thief took all of my dad's tools. It's hard to be a mechanic when you don't have tools to work with, and replacing everything was expensive.

My parents did their best to protect me and my siblings from the financial challenges, and they made sure we had all of the important things in life—a roof over our heads, food on the table, love and support. But we could tell it was weighing on them.

So, that Christmas, my siblings and I scrounged up whatever extra money we had made from shoveling driveways and babysitting. After all the presents had been opened, we gave them one last gift—a card with the money inside it, and a note telling them to go out for dinner, just the two of them. It wasn't much, but we wanted a chance to take care of our parents, the same way they took care of us.

Despite a few challenges, my parents never wavered in their generosity. And neither did the people around us. A lot of our tournaments required long road trips and overnight stays. Without the help of Brian's parents, it would have been tough for me to play in a lot of them. My parents had to work a lot of weekends to keep making ends meet, and they couldn't afford the cost or time to drive me and my siblings everywhere we needed to be, no matter much they wanted to. Brian's parents often stepped in, never hesitating to take me along with them and Brian, whether we were driving to the next town over or up into Canada for a weekend of competition. My parents chipped in whenever they could, and we were all grateful for the help; we were like one, big extended family.

When my mom did take me and my siblings to our games, she had one rule: the first time we forgot a piece of equipment at home, she'd go get it for us. But she'd only do it one time. She would get us to games all over the state, but the responsibility was on us to make sure that we had everything we needed to play once we got there.

It was during my PeeWee year in hockey, when I was eleven years old, that things started to get really interesting. That year, a Russian team came to town to play in a friendly tournament. Each family billeted some of the Russian kids who stayed with us during the tournament. As a thank-you gift, one of the kids whom we hosted gave me a Russian hockey stick. It was a wood stick with Russian lettering down the side, and it had a wicked toe curve at the end of the blade.

I started using the stick on the ice right away, and my first slap shot with it took off harder and higher than I'd ever shot before. *I can get used to this*, I thought.

Our team did really well that year, and at the end of the season, my mom put my trophy on a shelf in the living room. I hated when she did that. I never wanted to brag or show off, and anytime I saw a photo of me or an article about one of our games on the fridge, I tried to take it down.

One trophy I was proud of, though, was the one we won at the ESSO Cup. When I was twelve, I was playing for two teams. I played for our town team, the Woonsocket North Stars, when we competed for state titles. At the same time, I also played for the Mass Bay Chiefs, an AAA rep team out of Boston, in showcase tournaments, like the ESSO Cup. Brian Boucher was our goalie that season, and we traveled to Toronto as part of the showcase team in the tournament.

We had a good squad. Tom Poti was there with us, and all of the kids were great at that age. But there was one reason we won the tournament: Brian. He stood on his head game after game and stole a few wins for us, including a tight one against the Detroit Little Caesars.

I ended up being named the MVP of that tournament. I cared less about the award itself than the fact that it was being given out by Don Cherry. I knew Don Cherry—my mom put a new *Rock 'Em, Sock 'Em* VHS in my stocking every Christmas—and I had always liked his suits.

As he presented me with the award, Don mentioned that he was really impressed with our team. I mumbled a shy thanks, but then he made my day when he said he liked how I played the game. I shook his hand, said thanks, and skated back to my teammates, a huge grin plastered on my face.

After the ESSO Cup, we went to the prestigious Silver Stick tournament, where the best youth hockey teams from across Canada and the United States went to play. We made it all the way to the finals, but we fell short. We were supposed to then play in the Quebec City International PeeWee tournament. But shortly after the Silver Stick tournament, we got some disappointing news: we'd been disinvited to the Quebec City competition.

It turns out the Quebec City organizers had seen us play and, well, we had some tough characters on our team. Guys like Ryan Coughlin and Joe Grey were from the tough, south end of Boston, and they fought in every single game. I remember watching Ryan going to the penalty box after one fight and a dad from the crowd was yelling at him. Ryan looked up at the guy and yelled through the glass, "You want to fight me, too? Let's go!" He was twelve years old.

The organizers of the Quebec PeeWee tournament didn't like the idea of a team full of tough Southies starting a brawl.

Rough hockey never bothered me at all. I liked the hitting. The more physical I played, the better that I played. When a guy on the other team tried to run me, I could feel my heart start to beat faster. Time would slow down, just for a moment, and I could hear my breath in my ears. Most of the time, it ended with the other guy on the ice and me skating off with the puck. It all made me feel more involved in the game.

Even though we didn't get to play in Quebec City, we were still the best team in the Woonsocket area the rest of that year and for several thereafter. In and around New England, we were beating teams by scores like 12–0 and 15–0. After a few too many blowout wins, we decided to make it fairer for the weaker teams. One of the other guys on the team and I would take turns playing goalie against the weaker teams, just to give Brian a break.

The highlight of my minor hockey career, though, took place in April 1990, when I was invited to Berlin, Germany, for the Friendship Tournament.

At the time, my dad and a gentleman by the name of Joe Cavanagh coached our team. Joe easily could have played in the NHL, he was that good of a player, but he'd become a lawyer instead. He still holds the record for the most points scored at the prestigious Beanpot tournament—the annual tournament held between the four major hockey schools of Boston—and was a well-known hockey figure in New England.

My dad and Coach Cavanagh put together an all-star team of kids in our age group from around Rhode Island, including Brian and my brother Greg, who was Brian's backup. Our official team name was the East Providence Blues.

The team didn't have any funding, so we had to do a ton of fundraising just to raise enough money to pay for the flights overseas. Flying a bunch of twelve- and thirteen-year-olds from Rhode Island to Berlin was a big deal back then.

Each weekend, we did something different for the community. We held car washes, pancake breakfasts, and dynamite dinners.

Dynamite dinners were a big deal in New England and the northeastern United States as a whole. They were an easy and affordable way to feed a lot of people. You rented a local function hall, scrounged up some raffle prizes, and served everyone a dynamite dinner—basically hamburger mixed in with onions and pepper and served on a torpedo roll.

We were amazed and humbled by the community's generosity. People would donate anywhere from five to a hundred dollars to help us out. Eventually we raised all the money, and, thanks to my mom's connections at the travel agency where she worked, we were on our way to Europe.

I don't remember too much about the hockey. I do remember being wide-eyed at all of the sights around me. The Berlin Wall had just come down a few months earlier, and the city was completely unlike anything I'd ever seen. On one of our off days, we took a trip to the Berlin Wall to see it for ourselves. While we were there, we chipped off small chunks of the wall to bring back with us. I stared down at the small, paint-flecked piece of stone in my hand, and I was awed by the thought that I was holding history in my palm.

When we got back to Woonsocket, my mom made Greg and me hand-deliver thank-you cards and a piece of the Berlin Wall to everyone who donated money or helped us with the fund-raising. It took a village to send us halfway around the world to play hockey; the least we could do was bring a bit of the world back home.

•   •   •

When I reached grade seven, I had a decision to make. I could keep going to the local middle school around the corner, or I could start new at Mount Saint Charles Academy.

It wasn't much of a decision, though—all I ever wanted to do was end up playing varsity hockey at the Mount.

Everyone in Woonsocket knew about Mount Saint Charles—it was the dominant school in town. It was a private Catholic school with a big-name reputation. And, most important, it was one of the best hockey schools in Rhode Island, maybe even in the entire United States.

I knew where I wanted to be. Hockey had become the main focus of my life, and I had my sights set not just on playing for Mount Saint Charles, but on one day making it to the NHL. When I arrived there, Mount Saint Charles's hockey team had won thirteen consecutive state titles, going back to 1978 (the streak would continue to 2003, earning the school twenty-six straight championships). Brian was planning on going there, too, and we knew that if we were going to make it to the big leagues, we had to play at the highest level we could.

I applied for the school and got in, and the first thing I did when I got there was sign up for tryouts for the hockey team. I made the team and never looked back.

Hockey quickly came to dominate my life. In grades seven and eight, along with the Mount Saint Charles Junior High team, I also still played for the Woonsocket North Stars and the Mass Bay Chiefs. By playing a few games for the Chiefs, I qualified to play in the big showcase tournaments when the team traveled to them. It was hard to manage the time needed for each team, so, like almost every other kid who played hockey in Rhode Island, I had what we called a "split season." Beginning in September, I would play fifteen games with the North Stars, then I'd take a break from that team when the school hockey season started around the end of November. After the school season—roughly thirty games—ended, I'd go back to playing for the North Stars. All of the other guys on the Mount Saint Charles team played on the Woonsocket North Stars team, too.

It added up, though, and when I entered grade nine, I stopped playing for the Chiefs. The North Stars and varsity hockey were more than enough to fill my time.

My second year of high school, I hit a growth spurt—I was six foot one and weighed 190 pounds. Needless to say, I was a lot bigger than most of the other kids my age. At practice, we would go through break-out drills where the forwards came into the zone on the forecheck while the defense tried to move the puck up the ice. I would pick up the puck in the corner, my mind going back to the positioning lessons my dad taught me. Then I took off, knocking the forwards out of the way. Guys eventually learned what I was doing and tried to hit me, but they'd just bounce off. I felt unstoppable.

I was a big believer in the idea that the best defense is a good offense. Thankfully, my coaches at Mount Saint Charles, Bill and Dave Belisle—a father-and-son duo—were there to remind me that I wouldn't always be able to skate around the problem. I had to keep working on the defensive part of my game if I was going to be able to compete at the highest levels.

"Bryan, you rush the puck up the ice so often, I'm not sure if you can even skate backward," Dave said, laughing.

Even though I loved rushing the puck, I knew Bill and Dave were right, and I tried to put their advice into action. It was a particularly timely lesson, because I soon learned that I definitely wasn't invincible.

Later that year, we were playing in a Hockey Night in Boston event being held at Merrimack College, just north of Boston.

I was playing for Team Rhode Island, and one of my teammates was a guy named Ryan Murphy. Ryan couldn't have been more than five feet, six inches tall, but he was a good hockey player, and a tough one, too. During the game, Ryan got in a beef with another player. I was on the ice at the same time, and I stood off to the side while the two of them engaged. They circled around each other, and once Ryan got a hold of the other guy's jersey, he started giving it to him pretty good. It seemed like your average hockey fight.

But as the two of them fell on the ice, I suddenly heard Ryan scream, "He's biting me!"

I immediately skated over and dragged the other kid off Ryan to make him stop biting. The refs didn't love that I was the third man in, though, and all three of us ended up getting kicked out of the game.

After the game, Ryan and I were walking with my mom back to the car when suddenly, six players—including the one who bit Ryan—and two of the dads from the other team appeared around us.

My mom stared at the kid who bit Ryan, then looked right in the eyes of one of the dads and said, "I hope your son has all of his shots."

The dad didn't take kindly to that. He got right in my mom's face and pushed her. Before I could do anything, Ryan punched the guy in the face.

In an instant, it was a parking lot donnybrook!

Growing up in Woonsocket, I always knew that, in a fight, you can never fall down. If you're on your feet, you can defend yourself and dole out some punishment. But once you fall down, you are in trouble.

Ryan and I were doing our best, but we were outnumbered. Thank God my mom was there. Out of the corner of my eye, I saw her leap on the back of one of the dads, trying to pull him away from Ryan.

We were making a ton of noise, and it wasn't long before the other Rhode Island fathers heard what was happening and came running out to help us. Once they showed up, the fight was over because they started kicking ass. One of the Rhode Island dads walked up to the guy who had shoved my mom and dropped him with one punch.

The other guys scattered after that. Ryan and I looked at each other, and we were a bloodied mess. As I got my bearings and watched the guys who attacked us walk across the parking lot, I realized that you could see the scratches from my mom's nails across their shirts.

My mom wanted to go the police, but I didn't want any part of that. We had got our asses kicked, and all I wanted was to go home. When we got home, my brother Greg looked at me and asked, "How's the other guy look?"

I shook my head. "Pretty rough, but not because of me." Greg looked at me, confused. "Just don't ever mess with Mom," I said.

•   •   •

I left Mount Saint Charles after grade ten and enrolled at a place called Tabor Academy in Marion, Massachusetts. Tabor was a prep school, and I had just made the USA Hockey Select-16 team, which was made up of the top recruited sixteen-year-olds from across the country.

The Tabor hockey coaches saw me play, and they recruited me, along with a bunch of other guys who went on to play pro hockey at various levels, like Deron Quint, E. J. Bradley, and Eric Nicholas.

The coach was a guy named Peter Herms, a young, up-and-coming hockey guy. We were all excited to play under him. But then, right before school was supposed to start, the Tabor Academy fired him.

I was in Colorado Springs, training with the Select-16 team, when I got the news. I immediately shared it with the rest of the guys who were supposed to go to Tabor. We didn't know who was lined up to replace Herms, who had been one of the main reasons we wanted to play there. It seemed the program at Tabor was going through some difficult times, and I suddenly got cold feet.

Luckily for me, Mount Saint Charles agreed to take me back for my junior year, so I didn't miss the season. I was back for only a couple of months, though, when I returned to the national team.

In November 1993, the USA Select-16's took part in the World Under–17 hockey challenge. That year the tournament was held in Amos, Quebec, a six-hour drive north of Montreal. To get there from Woonsocket meant we were on the road well over ten hours.

Despite the long haul, both of my parents drove up to Amos so they could watch the tournament. This was November, so while it was getting cold in Rhode Island, it wasn't horrible. Amos, Quebec, though, was freezing cold.

My dad totally underestimated how cold it would get at night.

His first night there, my dad noticed everyone else was plugging their car into a heater for the night. He didn't have a heater available, so he lifted the hood and put blankets over the motor, then closed everything up, hoping that would work.

It didn't. When we woke in the morning, the motor was completely frozen over. My dad had to get his car towed to the nearest garage, where they installed a block heater. He was thrilled when the tournament ended a few days later and we could drive back to Rhode Island.

I kept playing for Mount Saint Charles throughout the rest of high school, but I was playing more and more for national teams in tournaments like the one in Quebec. In fact, Brian Boucher and I might be the only kids from Woonsocket who ended up in a hockey tournament in Mexico.

I was part of the USA Select-17's that won a silver medal at a tournament held in La Copa, Mexico. The year before, Brian had been battling some nagging injuries, so he hadn't made the Select-16's. I was thrilled, then, when he recovered from his injuries and also made the Select-17's that year.

If I'd thought Berlin was different from my hometown, Mexico City was a whole other story. I'd always known my family wasn't rich, but the poverty we saw in Mexico City was unlike anything I'd seen. On the drive to the rink, we saw families living in small sheds by the river. I reminded myself that I was lucky and privileged to have all of the luxuries I did.

We got to the rink for our first practice and started warming up. We were still jet-lagged, so we just wanted to get our legs moving.

But the first shot someone took went high over the net. It struck the glass above the boards, and broke it.

The guy who took the shot let out a whoop. "Boys, did you see that bomb of a shot?" he bragged.

The rest of us looked at each other with our eyebrows raised—it hadn't been that hard a shot. Then somebody else fired a puck that hit the glass, and sure enough, that pane broke, too.

We skated over to get a closer look, and we realized the organizers had used real glass around the boards of the arena!

We grinned at each other, and the next thing you knew, the pucks were flying and glass was shattering all over the rink. It took us less than a minute to break every single glass panel around the boards. By the time the coaches made it to the ice, they had to cancel practice because there were shards of glass all over it. We got chewed out by the coaches afterward for being so destructive, but as carefree seventeen-year-olds, we felt it was worth it.

Once the games started (and the boards were fixed), we quickly got serious. The tournament was a good test against top talent from Canada, Finland, and a bunch of other countries. We were playing against guys that we had read about in *The Hockey News*.

We were good, but the Canadian teams were just better than us. Canada entered three separate teams in this tournament—one each from the West, Ontario, and Quebec. They were stocked with good players—guys like Wade Redden, Jarome Iginla, and Shane Doan. We tried our best to keep up with them, but they were a step above.

The tournament didn't end with us raising a trophy, but it was still eye-opening for me. I'd finally seen up close just how skilled the best players my age could be. I wanted to be one of them. I wanted to follow the same path they were taking, straight to the NHL. If I was going to do that, though, I couldn't stay at Mount Saint Charles. It was time to take the next step—major junior hockey awaited.

2

GETTING AN EDUCATION

ABOUT HALFWAY THROUGH MY TIME AT MOUNT SAINT CHARLES, I TOLD MY parents my new goal.

"I want to play major junior hockey," I said to them as we sat around the dinner table.

My parents exchanged glances. "We've been through this before," my mom said. "You need to go to college."

"But, Mom," I said, "those Canadian guys I was playing against are all going to the NHL. If I'm going to be drafted, I have to be playing against guys like them. I can only do that in the OHL."

"And you can," she said. "As long as you get an education first."

"What if I at least try out for the Junior Red Wings as an underage player?" I said, hoping to negotiate a bit.

"No," my mom said firmly. "You're finishing high school."

Most American kids saw college hockey as the obvious next step after high school. But having seen how good the Canadian guys were, I was convinced that the Ontario Hockey League was my best chance of being drafted to the NHL.

At the Select-16's and Select-17's, I had played against guys like Jason Doig, Jerome Iginla, Shane Doan, and Wade Redden. The caliber of the hockey at those tournaments convinced me that I wanted to play junior hockey. I just hoped I had what it would take.

Playing at Mount Saint Charles had been fun, but I had gone as far as I could go there. We were still regularly blowing out teams by huge scores. One night, we were playing my younger brother Greg's school, and we were pounding them. Late in the game, my dad looked across the rink at me from the stands. He just stared me down while I was on the bench. I got his message loud and clear: *Take it easy on your younger brother.* I knew it was time to cool it.

Over the next few weeks, I begged and pleaded and negotiated. But my parents held firm—I wouldn't be allowed to try out for the OHL unless I finished all of my high school credits first.

The rest of that year was a total blur. Each day, I got up early and headed to hockey practice at the school first thing. I'd go to a full load of classes during the day, and then, in the evenings, I went to a local community college to get my extra credits—History on Mondays and Wednesdays, English on Tuesdays and Thursdays. Fridays and weekends, I'd play baseball with the varsity team.

One of the last things I had to do before I could graduate from Mount Saint Charles was write a thesis paper for our religion class. In it, I had to explain how my upbringing had influenced my life and what my future goals were.

I decided to write from the heart. I talked about how hardworking my parents were and how I'd learned from them the importance of keeping an open door to the family, friends, and community around me. I mentioned the community that had supported me along the way, from dynamite dinners to the Boucher's driving me to and from tournaments. I talked about how grateful I was for everything and everyone who had brought me to that point, and how it made me determined to never give up on my dream of making the NHL.

It was tough balancing everything over those months, but I was able to pull it off. That spring, I earned my high school diploma. I was free to play in the OHL.

I immediately turned my focus back to hockey full-time. My first glimpse of the OHL came in Detroit. My parents and I flew to Detroit to see the Junior Red Wings play a game at the Joe Louis Arena. The arena was famous, even then, and the moment I walked through the doors, I craned my neck up to look at the banners hanging from the ceiling, each and every one of them marking a legendary player or team. The game itself had everything—it was a flurry of scoring, hitting, and fighting. The crowd was shouting and cheering the entire time, and the big screen played replays during the breaks. The guys on the ice were barely older than me, but it felt like they were playing in a pro game. I knew I was hooked.

I wanted to play for the Junior Red Wings in Detroit, but other teams started to get wind that I was interested in junior. I was ranked in the top three prospects in the OHL draft that year, but Detroit had the ninth pick overall. I'm sure I would have been happy playing for one of the other teams in the league, but I had my sights set on Detroit, and nothing was going to dissuade me.

So, my parents and I reached out to Mike Milbury, who had just been hired at Boston College. The idea came from my agent at the time, Mark Peroni. Mark was my agent for only a short period, but he had a strategy for how we could make everything work.

By that point, I had all of my high school credits and we signed a letter of intent with Boston College. I was seventeen—still a year younger than most of the guys heading to college—but we figured that if I didn't end up getting drafted by the Detroit Junior Red Wings, I could go to Boston College, realizing my dreams of playing higher-level hockey and my parents' of sending me to college.

We explained the situation to Mike, and I signed a letter of intent saying that I was going to play at Boston College as a seventeen-year-old freshman.

Once the Junior teams heard that, none of them were willing to risk their first-round pick on me, as they figured I was going to play at Boston College.

But Jim Rutherford, the GM of the Junior Red Wings, decided it was worth the risk, and in the spring of 1994, the Junior Red Wings drafted me ninth overall. My hard work had paid off—I was going to the OHL.

•   •   •

As much as I was desperate to play junior hockey, it was still the great unknown for me when I arrived at training camp. I didn't know what to expect or how the hockey would compare to what I'd experienced at Mount Saint Charles.

It took me only a few shifts to realize this was a big step up from anything I'd ever experienced. Every player on the ice had been the best wherever they came from. You couldn't coast, or phone in your effort. The second you did, you'd be plastered against the boards or find the puck in the back of your net.

Bringing together a bunch of young players who have never met each other and getting them to work together can be tricky. Luckily, we had exactly the right coach for the task in Paul Maurice.

Paul knew when to praise us and when to kick us in the butt and get us going. He could motivate us to perform well on the ice, but he also understood where each of us was coming from. Like a lot of other guys on the team, I was a seventeen-year-old kid living away from home for the first time. A few weeks earlier, I'd had all of the comforts and routines of home. Now I was trying to find out where I fit not just on the team, but in the wider world around me.

That was a big reason that Paul paired me on the blue line with Jamie Allison, an older and more mature defenseman.

The first time I met Jamie, we shook hands in the dressing room and he said, "So, you're the American hotshot, eh?"

I didn't know what to say. I'd never met anyone on the team before, and I certainly hadn't bragged about my time in Rhode Island. Had a rumor spread about me already?

Suddenly Jamie grinned. "Relax, man, I'm kidding. Welcome to the Red Wings!"

I quickly learned that Jamie liked to tease a lot, but that he would always have my back. Jamie protected me a lot of times, both on and off the ice, and I will always appreciate that.

The first time I saw Jamie fight, I could see right away how tough he was. He was throwing punches with both hands, and he just stood there and took whatever the other guy threw at him. In that era of the

OHL, there were some tough characters all over the league, and Jamie could more than hold his own with all of them.

But Jamie was more than just a tough guy; he could also move the puck, and he was a solid player. I really liked playing with him. The two of us logged a lot of ice time together. He was a smart, stay-at-home defenseman, which allowed me the freedom to play my game. And with Jamie's reputation around the league, guys around the OHL knew not to mess with me because I was riding shotgun with Jamie.

Our whole team was tight like that. Every day in the locker room, and every trip on the team bus, was full of jokes and getting up to some kind of trouble. When we went on long road trips, a few guys would inevitably sneak some rye or beer onto the bus. Other guys would roll cigarettes and pop the emergency exit hatch on the roof to let out the smoke. We had no money; whenever we played cards on the bus, guys would bet tins of tobacco. Anytime the bus took a corner, a bunch of empty water bottles now filled with tobacco juice would clatter across the floor. It was a long way from the pristine home my family had kept. Just the smell of the tobacco juice in those bottles was enough to make me sick.

A couple of hours into the trip, I'd inevitably hear the jokes starting. I was a rookie, so the team hierarchy dictated that I sit at the front of the bus with the other first-years.

"Hey, Bryan, you going to scoar-ah tonight?" someone would call from the back, mimicking my accent.

"You ready to skate hard, Bernie?" another asked. The guys had started calling me "Bernie" ever since Paul Maurice had jokingly asked whether there was an *n* in "Berard." I went along with it—if the coach wanted to call me Bernie, then I'd be Bernie. It wasn't as though I had much of a choice—once Paul started calling a player by a nickname, he kept calling them by it all year long.

The chirping was always harmless like that, and as always, Jamie had my back, making sure it never went too far. It was our way of testing each other, making sure we all had the kind of character we looked for in a teammate, and exploring what kinds of young adults we wanted to be.

That was especially important that year, because it became clear we had a talented team and that we were poised to make a deep run in the playoffs. And by teasing each other all the time, we made ourselves immune to the chirps we heard on the ice. Every time we played, guys on the other team would chirp me to try to get me off my game. It always had the opposite effect—it made me play harder, and I made a point to stand up for myself to the guys around me and prove that I belonged in the OHL.

My first fight in the OHL was against Wayne Primeau in Owen Sound. And the best part about it was that my parents were there to see it. My mom and dad had flown to Detroit, and my new agent, Tom Laidlaw, picked them up and drove them to Owen Sound to see us play. Tom was taking my parents around to a few different rinks in the OHL so they would see where I was playing all those months that I was living away from home.

Wayne was a lot bigger than me, and when we squared off, I realized he had a long reach on me. It would have been easy to realize my mistake and just turtle, going down to avoid getting hit too much. But out of the corner of my eye, I saw my teammates gathered around the bench to watch the showdown. *Time to show them what I've got*, I thought, cocking back my fist.

The fight didn't go well for me—I landed maybe one square punch, and Primeau beat me up pretty good. But as I skated over to the penalty box, all I could hear were the taps of my teammates' sticks on the ice. It was music to my ears.

My parents had seen me fight before, both on and off the ice, so when I saw my dad after the game, he had a big smile on my face. He was proud that I had held my own against a bigger opponent like Primeau.

When I was growing up, my dad was known as being a tough guy in Woonsocket. I still hear stories about him to this day. Sometimes he'd tease me and say, "You wish you were as tough as me, kid." He wasn't wrong, but I knew I didn't have a future of winning hockey fights ahead of me.

Still, the fight helped earned me a bit more respect from my teammates. The next day on the bus ride back to Detroit, I didn't hear a single joke from the back of the bus directed at me.

That 1994–95 season was unique in the OHL. There was a lockout in the NHL that year, so a lot of guys who would have been playing in the NHL came back to play in the OHL. That's why Jamie Allison was playing with us that year, and the same went for Todd Harvey. If it weren't for the lockout, both would have been playing pro hockey that season. I felt bad that those guys had to wait another year for their shot at the big leagues, but I did appreciate that it made the competition that year in the OHL all the more intense.

The intensity of the hockey and of my new life in Detroit took a bit of a toll on me that first year. I was homesick and worn down. In high school, I had played twenty-five or thirty games a year. But in the OHL, we were traveling to sixty-six games, not including the playoffs.

It was more hockey in a season than I'd ever had before, even when I was playing for three teams at once.

Halfway through the season, Paul pulled me into his office for a talk. I was feeling sorry for myself, but if I expected Paul to feel the same, I was sorely mistaken.

"Bryan, do you want to be here?" Paul asked.

"What do you mean?" I said, my confusion spread across my face.

"I mean, do you want to play in the OHL?"

"Of course," I said. "I want to make it to the NHL."

"Then you need to smarten up," Paul said. He proceeded to chew me out, telling me that if I was serious about a career in hockey, I had to stop feeling sorry for myself and start to pick up my play. Lots of guys wanted to make it to the NHL—it was the ones who were willing to sacrifice everything who would get there.

It worked. I went back to the team with a new focus and determination to give my best every single day.

When I needed a break, I could always retreat to my billet family's house. My teammate Sean Haggerty and I were living with a great family, the Coules, that season. Tom and Lynn took great care of us. They had a young son and daughter, and they warmly welcomed us into their home as though we were their own kids. They had a finished basement that they turned into a hangout spot for Sean and me.

Tom and Lynn lived on Gros Isle, a little island downriver from Detroit. It was a quiet little town, and Sean and I didn't mind being a little outside of Detroit. All of us on the team were spread throughout the city's suburbs. Some of them even lived across the border in Windsor.

Because we were so spread out, Joe Louis Arena became the

central gathering place for our team. It was our beating heart. We played there, practiced there, and hung out in our spare time there.

I was a total rink rat that first year. I didn't have to worry about going to high school, like a lot of other guys. I was taking a class at the University of Michigan—my mom was still big on me getting an education, and I wanted to show her I was doing something. I called my parents as often as I could. I would tell them how I was doing, but I was more interested in hearing how everyone else was doing back in Woonsocket. That meant more to me, to know that everyone back home was doing well.

But after that one semester, I spent nearly all my spare time at the rink. I would either be watching the Red Wings practice or playing some shinny when the ice was free. There were a few of us on the Red Wings who were done with high school—me, Jamie Allison, Scott Blair, and my billet roommate, Sean Haggerty—so when other guys were at school, we were at the rink. Most afternoons, we'd throw on some sweatpants, shin pads, skates, and gloves and play shinny with a tennis ball instead of a puck. It was a way to blow off steam, but it also let us work on our hand-eye coordination.

Because I spent so much time around the rink, I got to know some of the Detroit Red Wings players. After a while, I felt like I'd seen them regularly enough to say hi and make some small talk whenever I had a chance.

One of the guys I chatted with the most was Paul Coffey. Paul was a major star in the NHL, yet he treated me and all the other junior players like we were equals. In fact, he turned out to be just as much of a rink rat as us junior players. We often saw Coffey and his German shepherd hanging around the rink, and he even joined in on our ball hockey games when he had a chance.

One day, as I was leaving the ice after practice, Paul came up to me and said, "Follow me."

We headed down the hallway, where the equipment guy from the Red Wings was waiting. At the time, I wore a size 9½ skate with a size 280 blade.

"Bryan needs a bigger skate blade on his boot," Paul said to the equipment manager.

"I do?" I said.

"You do," said Paul. Paul's theory was that, if I had a bigger blade, I would be able to generate more glide speed in my stride—the more blade on the ice, the faster I could go. I watched as the Red Wing's equipment manager installed size 288 blades into my skates, and then I headed back on the ice.

Damn, I thought after the first few strides. *Paul knew what he was talking about.*

"This is amazing!" I shouted across the ice as Paul watched from the boards. He gave a wave and headed out. I ended up using the same skate setup the rest of my career, and every time I got new blades on my skate, I remembered how grateful I was to Paul for taking the time to help a younger player.

Being around the Red Wings all the time lit a fire under my butt to work harder and get better every day. The Red Wings carried themselves in such an impressive manner—it showed me what professional hockey was all about.

Between Paul Maurice's motivation and Coffey's advice, I noticed my game starting to improve. Late in the season, the league held a skills competition, and I was invited to participate. I was there to have a good time and learn a bit from the guys around me, but I ended up having the hardest shot, and I won the award as the fastest skater as well. I was using a wooden stick, and they measured my shot at ninety-seven miles per hour. And then I clocked a 13.7-second lap in the fastest skater competition.

Not long after the skills competition I was invited to the CHL All-Star Challenge. Paul Maurice was coaching our team, and the Kitchener Memorial Auditorium was packed full of fans and NHL scouts. My dad came to the game, and he was thrilled when he found out he'd be sitting beside Walter Gretzky, father of Wayne Gretzky. It wasn't just luck that made it happen—my agent, Tom Laidlaw, worked for the head of the IMG hockey agency at the time, and was a longtime friend of Wayne's agent, Mike Barnett. My dad and Walter got along great, although I'm not sure how my dad explained the fight I got into with Terry Ryan during the game. It was a wild tilt—Kevin Weekes was our goalie, and as I fought Ryan, Weekes was coaching me on what punches to throw.

When I rejoined the Red Wings, I was feeling confident about my game, as did the other guys on the team. We felt we had a team that could win it all, and we set out to do exactly that.

We were undefeated in our first two series of the playoffs, steam-rolling over London and Peterborough. We played Sudbury in the semifinals, and the series was tight, going all the way to game 7. Nobody expected us to even get that far, and we shook things up when we beat Sudbury in seven games. That set us up for a match-up against Guelph in the OHL Finals.

Guelph were the favorites—they were the top team in the league that season, and they hadn't lost a single playoff game heading into the finals. They were stacked with talented future NHLers like Todd

Bertuzzi and Jeff O'Neill. Counting myself, only a few guys on the Junior Red Wings went to play in the NHL. Meanwhile the Storm were loaded with talent.

It was a long, tough series, but we found a way to beat them 5–4 in game 6 to win it all. It was one of those games where it felt like the puck was on my stick all night. I just knew we were going to get it done and we did. I was proud to score the winning goal, but I was prouder to be part of something special. The Detroit Junior Red Wings had just become the first American team to win the OHL championship.

We had done what everyone thought was impossible, and we had the OHL championship under our belts.

But we weren't done yet. Not long after celebrating our win over Guelph, we started getting ready for the Memorial Cup, a weeklong tournament to determine the champion of the Canadian Hockey League.

We were representing the OHL that year, and we were going up against the Hull Olympiques, the QMJHL champs, the Brandon Wheat Kings, who had won the WHL, and the Kamloops Blazers, the hosts.

The whole Kamloops area was so beautiful. It was one of the nicest Junior towns I had ever been to, and they had a brand-new rink to play in.

We had a few days off just before the tournament, and a bunch of us went an hour north of Kamloops to this beautiful little lake to do some trout fishing. We floated around in inner tubes and fly-fished all day long.

Being not-so-bright teenagers, we didn't realize how hard fly-fishing and inner tubing around the lake would be on our legs. The next day, our calf muscles were absolutely killing us. It wasn't the smartest way to start the Memorial Cup, but it was a great team-bonding moment.

After our break, we got serious again about the games ahead. If I'd thought the OHL playoffs were intense, this was somehow a step above even that. I knew most of the top players on the other teams—guys like Wade Redden and Shane Doan—because I had been playing against them in tournaments since I was sixteen years old. And I knew that we had to bring our best if we were going have any hope of beating them.

At the start of the Memorial Cup, I weighed around 195 pounds and was six foot one. When I hit my top gear, I was flying out there. I had the kind of speed that could get me in and out of trouble anywhere on the ice. Guys on other teams jokingly called me the "Rocket from Woonsocket."

I didn't pay attention to the names, though. Paul Maurice had entrusted Jamie and me with shutting down the top guys on the other teams, and that required all of my discipline and energy, as Jamie and I were playing anywhere from thirty-five to forty minutes a night.

We did well enough in the round robin to make it to the semifinals, where we beat Wade Redden and the Brandon Wheat Kings 2–1. That meant we'd be facing the Kamloops Blazers in the finals.

I had injured myself in the semifinal game against Brandon. I took a knee coming across center ice, and I ended up with a big-time charley horse and a contusion in my leg. The night before the finals, the doctors and the training staff tried everything to get me ready. They even used a big needle to try to drain the blood out of my charley horse.

The trainers were worried that I would wake up stiff when I went to bed. They wanted me to sleep with my knee at a ninety-degree angle so that I wouldn't roll onto the injury. So before I went to bed, they taped my ankle to my thigh to keep my knee bent all night.

The next morning, I was still feeling the charley horse, so they went back to the needle to try to draw out more blood. None of it helped at all, and I eventually accepted that I would have to play the final game on basically one leg.

I was far from perfect, but I tried to put the pain out of my mind. I had to—we were about to play the best team in junior hockey.

Even if we had been 100 percent healthy, though, we were underdogs against the Kamloops team. They had Jarome Iginla, Shane Doan, Darcy Tucker, Jason Strudwick—the list went on. They were a junior hockey dynasty. The year before, they had repeated as Memorial Cup champions, and that game, they showed us why they were champions. We put up the best fight we could, but Kamloops beat us 8–2, winning the title for the third time in the four years.

Even though we lost, I was grateful to have the experience. I thought back to how far I'd come in just a couple of years since I first saw these guys play. I was starting to understand what it took in terms of mental and physical discipline to play with the best of the best. I'd had a taste, and I wanted more.

3

THE DRAFT

IN JULY 1995, MY ENTIRE FAMILY—MY PARENTS, TWO OLDER SIBLINGS, AND three younger siblings—joined me in Edmonton for the annual NHL Entry Draft.

We all arrived two days before the draft to get settled in and be ready for the big day.

We wanted to be early so that we could enjoy the occasion. But I also had to meet with a few teams that were still making up their mind about the draft.

Before we'd even left Woonsocket, a couple of officials from the Ottawa Senators—Randy Sexton, the president and general manager, and John Ferguson, the chief scout—came to my parents' house to talk to me. There was no draft combine back then, so prospects and teams had to meet one-on-one to gauge each other's interest. Central

Scouting had ranked me in the top ten players for that year's draft, along with many of the guys I'd played against in the previous year in the CHL, including Shane Doan, Jarome Iginla, Chad Kilger, Daymond Langkow, and Kyle McLaren.

Once all the team meetings were out of the way in Edmonton, most of my time was spent fulfilling press and media obligations. In the quieter moments in between, though, I was able to enjoy some quality time with my family.

Before I knew it, the day of the draft arrived. I woke up that morning, expecting it to feel entirely different or for my stomach to be doing flips, but I was surprisingly calm. Having my family around helped. We had a big breakfast together and joked around with each other before piling into the car to head to the Edmonton Coliseum, where the draft was being held.

On the ride over, I thought about what the day might bring. I was so competitive that I felt that being selected first overall would be a huge accomplishment. Less so for me than for the United States. There were only two other Americans who had been drafted first overall in the NHL draft up to that point—Brian Lawton in 1983 and Mike Modano in 1988. I had met Brian Lawton at a sports banquet in Woonsocket as a kid, and I remembered how much I looked up to him at the time, this player who had been the first to rise to those heights. The idea of contributing to that legacy sent shivers down my spine.

My agent, Tom Laidlaw, was there with us, and he could tell what I was thinking.

"I think you'll go first overall," he said.

"We don't know that," I said. "There are a lot of amazing players in the draft." There was a lot of speculation that defensemen would go first, second, and third overall in the draft, but none of us knew what order we'd fall in.

"True," he said. "But I've just got a feeling."

I grinned. Tom had been my agent for so long, he was basically a family member, and I was grateful for his confidence. Over the years, he had basically become my sports psychologist. If I had a tough game, I could call him and talk over the things that were bothering me. Tom was a tough defenseman who played more than seven hundred games in the NHL for the Rangers and the Kings. I respected his advice, and I listened to whatever he had to say.

We finally settled into our seats, and I scanned the room for the teams I'd met with. The Senators had the top overall pick, but I also saw the flags for the rest of the teams with the top five picks in the draft—the Islanders, Kings, Ducks, and Lightning. *I could end up playing for any one of them*, I thought.

The crowd quieted down as Randy Sexton from the Ottawa Senators approached the stage. Sexton didn't waste any time.

"Welcome, great fans of Edmonton," he said. "The Ottawa Senators are pleased and proud to select with the first pick overall this year from the Detroit Junior Red Wings, Bryan Berard."

As soon as Sexton announced my name, the first thing I did was stand up and give my parents a big hug. I could barely hear anything over the applause of the crowd, but I managed to shout "Thank you" over and over in both of their ears. My parents had sacrificed so much for me to play hockey. I knew that hearing my name called that day was thanks to them, more than anyone else.

I walked down the aisle in front of my siblings, returning each of their smiles as I walked to the stage. I took off my jacket just before

I reached the stage, and the applause ramped up again as I took my place beside the Senators' officials onstage. I pulled on the black, red, and white jersey, curved the brim of the baseball hat they handed me, and turned to the cameras lined up at the front of the stage.

The flash from the cameras was blinding, but I kept trying to look up to where my family sat in the stands. This was a dream come true, and I was completely overcome by the excitement I was feeling, but I wanted to make sure they knew that this was their moment as much as mine.

The hubbub didn't stop after I left the stage. The rest of the day was a flurry of handshakes, interviews, and photo ops. I saw the other draft picks and their families milling around me, but we were all being pulled in a thousand different directions at once, so it was hard to catch my breath.

"Brian!" I shouted late in the day as I saw Brian Boucher and his parents go by. Brian had been drafted twenty-second overall by the Philadelphia Flyers.

"Congrats, man!" he said. "First overall—that's amazing."

"Same to you," I said. "Philly's a great team."

To this day, one of my most prized possessions is a photo of the two of us at the draft. Brian has his Flyers jersey on, and I'm wearing my Sens draft-day hat. Two kids from little Woonsocket, Rhode Island, who had just been drafted in the first round of the NHL.

We talked with each other's parents quickly and made plans to catch up later that night. After dinner with my family, I joined Brian and the other draft picks at a place called Barry T's, where we all had a drink to celebrate (we were making the most of the fact that Alberta's drinking age was eighteen). I had a 5 a.m. flight to Ottawa the next day, so it was an early night for me.

Before I knew it, my parents and I were touching down in Ottawa in the dawn light. We headed to a TV studio, where I had to do a morning interview. I liked what I saw of the city, especially how half the city spoke French—it reminded me of home. Then the Senators' officials took us on a tour of the new arena, Corel Centre, they were building. I thought of skating out onto the ice for the first time, my name on the Jumbotron as I took my place in the NHL. I was one step closer to seeing my dream come true.

•   •   •

After the NHL draft, I headed back to Woonsocket for a few weeks to relax. Before I knew it, though, the summer had flown by, and in September 1995, I headed back to Ottawa for the Senators' training camp. I immediately realized that I was now playing hockey with a bunch of men, not boys. And there is a very big difference.

I had spent the summer training and trying to get myself into shape. I thought I was in the best shape I could be. But when I came off the ice after one practice, we all had to do this workout on the exercise bike. I started pedaling and after a few minutes, I was wheezing, my lungs burning. I looked over at the veterans—if they were in pain, they weren't showing it. I tried to make it look easy, like they did, but I could tell I had some catching up to do.

The first time that you step on the ice with NHL-caliber players, it is a real shock. I was eighteen years old, and right away, I could tell the speed and the strength of the NHL game was different than anything that I had ever experienced. Still, I wanted to play in the NHL that year, and I felt I had the talent and the toughness to make it.

It was proving to be a tough transition, though. The Sens themselves were in a transitionary period. I came from a junior team where we were all pretty tight and there were no cliques to worry about. But I was noticing that the Senators' locker room was quite separate. There seemed to be small groups of guys, all pitted against each other. I was still a teenager, and even I noticed it right away.

It wasn't that the guys on the Sens were bad. It just didn't feel like a team to me, and there was a lack of communication between the team and the players.

It didn't help that my agent Tom Laidlaw was having some difficulty sorting out my contract with the Senators' management. The Sens were confident I was going to make the team, and that I could crack the lineup. But Tom found out that signing me wasn't in their budget for that year, and they couldn't afford to pay my signing bonus.

The whole dispute never should have happened, and the negotiation should have been straightforward. It was the first year of the rookie salary cap. I was set to make $850,000, and I had some bonus clauses available to me as well. I could make money if I scored a certain number of points, for example, if I was nominated for awards, or if I made the all-rookie team at the end of the year. The only way that I would make any of my bonuses would be if I achieved the goals written into the contract. None of them were guaranteed. That all seemed fair to me—if I performed at a high level and hit all the clauses in the contract, I could make more money.

But when that first bonus set in and the team couldn't pay it, it made us nervous. Tom and I had a series of long, difficult conversations. Ultimately, we both agreed that getting out of Ottawa was the best thing for me and for my career.

The fallout from that decision was ugly. Neither Tom nor I realized how bad it would get with the Ottawa press and fans. The impression was that I was a spoiled American kid who didn't want to play in Ottawa. This was shortly after Eric Lindros refused to play for the Quebec Nordiques and ended up being traded to the Flyers in a blockbuster deal.

I was devastated. I had just been playing in the Ontario Hockey League, and it wasn't as though I didn't want to play in Canada. If anything, the complete opposite was true. I'd seen how good Canadian teams could be, and I wanted to be a part of that.

I had a dream of playing with the best of the best, and I was determined to see that through. But in the back of my mind, I also knew that I had a responsibility. My parents had sacrificed so much to get me to that point. I wanted to be able to repay them for everything they'd done for me and take care of them and our family if things got worse back in Woonsocket. To me, that meant making sure I had the most successful career possible.

I had a conversation with my agent, Tom Laidlaw, and we decided that it would be better for me to leave the Sens' camp early and go back to junior.

So, after talking it over with Tom, I did just that, and left the Sens' camp early. I was too young to play in the AHL, which meant I had no choice but to go back and play in the OHL. So I went back to Detroit, where the team had been renamed the Junior Whalers. My plan was to hone my game and get stronger while Tom and the Senators worked things out.

I tried to look on the bright side, and I hoped to pick up right where we'd left off the previous season in Detroit. But even there, change was afoot. Our team name was changed from the Junior Red Wings to the Whalers, and we weren't allowed to play out of Joe Louis Arena anymore. There seemed to be some kind of break between our team's management and that of the Detroit Red Wings. The new name didn't bother me, but I was disappointed by the change in arena. Instead of absorbing lessons from the NHL players in the legendary arena, I'd be splitting games between a rink in Oak Park, Michigan, and the home arena of the Pistons, the Palace, in Auburn Hills, Michigan.

All of that jumping around and uncertainty took a toll on the team. We still played well, but we didn't have the same kind of chemistry that we'd had the previous year, when Joe Louis had been our home.

By December 1995, as the World Juniors were starting in Massachusetts, I was still waiting for the Senators to trade me. Tom told me that, under the rules of the collective bargaining agreement at the time, one option was for me to play two more years of junior hockey, at which point I could go back into the draft. Two more years in junior seemed like far too long. I was ready to make my move to the NHL now, and I didn't want to fall behind the other guys in my draft year.

Pierre Gauthier was now the GM of the Sens, and during the World Juniors, he and Tom had a sit-down. Tom proposed to Pierre that, instead of getting nothing for me by letting me stay in Junior, the Sens should make a deal and get something for me. We both knew the Sens didn't like the idea of trading their number-one pick, and I didn't like the idea of being traded from a team I'd never played for, but I still felt this was the best solution.

The stress was starting to get to me. One night, when we were playing Sarnia at the old Oak Park Arena, I heard Mark Hunter, Sarnia's coach, chirping me from the bench. His team had been running me all night long, so when I heard Mark chirping me, I started giving it right back. We went back and forth, shouting at each other, before I finally skated over to my bench.

I didn't know it at the time, but Mike Milbury, then the general manager of the New York Islanders, was watching that game. I guess he liked the way I was putting up a fight to Hunter, because Mike started showing up at more and more of my games over the next few weeks. I had been friendly with Mike since the time that my parents and I signed the letter of intent with him at Boston College. And the more I saw him at my games, the more I began to suspect there might be a move in my future.

On January 23, 1996, my suspicions were confirmed: the Senators traded me to the New York Islanders. I was being sent to Long Island along with Don Beaupre and Martin Straka, and the Sens ended up with Damian Rhodes and Wade Redden, who had been selected immediately after me in the draft.

I felt such relief when I heard the news, knowing I would have a place to go after I finished my second year in the OHL with Detroit. I immediately called my parents to share the good news.

"That means we can come see you play more," my dad said excitedly. He couldn't wait to hop in his car, drive to Long Island, and watch me play.

I was just as happy, because being closer to home meant that I could drive home for Christmas during the holidays. Our family bonds were as tight as ever, and I was glad I would have a chance to spend more time with them.

The rest of my OHL season had its ups and downs. We were eliminated in the semifinals of the playoffs by the Peterborough Petes, who went on to win the league championship. After the season, I was named the OHL defenseman of the year and the CHL defenseman of the year. It was an incredible honor.

After the season ended, I knew that I was ready for the next step in my hockey career. My mom had always talked about me going to college. When it comes to getting a young player ready to play in the NHL, the OHL is like taking a college-level course in how to play in the Show. I might not have spent much time in the classroom the past year, but I had received one heck of an education. Now it was time to put it to use.

4

A ROOKIE IN THE SHOW

THE SECOND I ARRIVED AT NASSAU VETERANS MEMORIAL COLISEUM, I FELT like I was home. It hit me when I headed into the Islanders' dressing room for the first time, and I could hear the room before I saw it. Everyone was chatting with each other, and I heard guys laughing and shouting each other's names. I immediately sensed I was where I needed to be.

The first thing that stood out to me when I entered the room at Islanders camp was just how many young players there were on the team, like Bryan McCabe, Todd Bertuzzi, Ziggy Palffy, Eric Fichaud, Marty McInnis, Travis Green, and Scott Lachance. I'd seen a lot of them in action over the years, and I knew that they were a great crop of players for anyone starting their career.

There were a number of veterans in the room, too, guys like Rich Pilon, Mick Vukota, and Derek King. A lot of them had grinded it out in the minors for years, fighting their way into the NHL. I gave those guys all the credit in the world, and I knew I had a lot to learn from them.

I did my best to settle into a rhythm with my new team. The returning players made it as easy as possible for new guys like me to adapt to life in the NHL. I was grateful for their guidance because the Islanders' organization was in a bit of flux when I got there, with the owners trying to sell the team. Mike Milbury was both the general manager and our head coach, and Rick Bowness—who had been the head coach of the Senators the year before when I attended training camp—was one of our associate coaches.

Rick was passionate about hockey, and sometimes his emotions got the better of him. He'd be giving you direction during a drill, and the next thing you knew, he would be screaming about something. I am not even sure if he knew he was doing it, he was just so determined to get the best out of everyone. I tried to keep my head down and focus on performing to the best of my abilities.

I felt great in the preseason, so when we headed out on a three-game road trip to start the 1996–97 season, I felt ready for whatever was coming. We touched down in Los Angeles, and all day leading up to my first game, I was buzzing with energy. The Islanders flew my parents from Rhode Island out to Los Angeles to watch me play my first game in the NHL—a classy move I was incredibly thankful for.

Knowing that my parents would be in the stands that night, and savoring the fact that I was finally making my debut in the big leagues, I was on cloud nine. As I stepped on the ice for our warm-ups, I could barely contain my energy. The air tasted crisper, and every sight and sound on the ice felt like it was dialed up.

Then the puck dropped and I got a reality check. I was shocked at the difference in tempo and intensity compared to the preseason. The game felt twice as fast and twice as physical. I would go to play the puck out of our corner, thinking I had a moment to get my bearings, and in that split second of hesitation, I'd find myself plastered against the boards or under pressure.

The league that year was full of guys who were terrifying, for various reasons. Mario Lemieux was a seemingly unstoppable scorer. He was coming off a season where he'd just scored 161 points. We played the Penguins back-to-back in the middle of the season, and he had seven assists in those two games alone.

And on the physical end of things, nothing was scarier than playing the Flyers in Philadelphia. The Legion of Doom—Eric Lindros, John LeClair, and Mikael Renberg—earned their nickname.

Lindros would hurt you in so many ways. He would crush you in the corner with a big hit. He would slash you with that big Bauer stick of his. He would muscle you out of the way in front of the net and bury the puck. Adding insult to injury, the Philadelphia fans would boo and heckle us all game long. I loved it, though—it made for a fun atmosphere.

I learned a little more about the league with each passing game.

Rich Pilon and Derek King each took me under their wing when I arrived on Long Island, and they were great mentors, both on and off the ice.

At the start of my rookie year, I was paired with Scott Lachance, or "LC" as we called him. After a while, though, I was paired with Dennis Vaske, and he patiently showed me how to bring my game up to the next level.

Vaske's guidance helped, and I slowly got a feel for the tempo of the NHL play. And I was rewarded with my first goal in November 1996. We were in Phoenix playing the Coyotes, who had just moved there from Winnipeg that season. Halfway through the first period, we were on the power play. Travis Green and Derek King worked the puck between them along the boards. Travis fed me a pass at the point, and I fired a slap shot that beat Nikolai Khabibulin.

I pumped my fist in the air as my teammates mobbed me. I was caught in celebrating the goal, so I completely forgot about the puck. It wasn't until I was back on the bench that I realized I'd forgotten to grab it as a memento. Fortunately, one of my teammates had grabbed it and given it safely to our trainers.

We had enough tough guys on our Islanders team that year that all of us younger players felt safe on the ice and had enough room to try to contribute offensively. Still, none of us wanted to rely on other guys fighting our battles for us. Sometimes push came to shove, and we have to be ready to push back.

My first NHL fight came on Boxing Day in 1996. It was late in the game, and we were up by a couple of goals. The Devils were getting frustrated, and after a whistle, someone cross-checked my teammate Ziggy Palffy in front of our net. Ziggy went down, and the rest of the guys looked around, wondering who'd done it. I saw the guy standing over Ziggy, and I didn't stop to think or see who it was. I just immediately skated over and cross-checked the guy back.

"What was that for?" I yelled.

He didn't say anything. He just turned around and dropped his gloves. As the guy reached toward me, I quickly threw my gloves and stick on the ground and looked up, and that's when I realized—the guy I'd cross-checked was Ken Daneyko. The same Ken Daneyko who once had 283 penalty minutes in one season and who was known by fans as "Mr. Devil." *Oh, boy,* I thought. *No backing out now.*

The guys on the bench started yelling, "Bryan, he's a lefty!"

By the time I heard them, I already knew what hand Daneyko punched with.

Daneyko hit me a few times right away, and one punch hit me in the helmet. Even though my helmet absorbed the worst of it, I could still feel the impact of his punch. *What are this guy's fists made of?* I wondered. I tried to throw a few punches of my own, then we fell to the ice. The linesmen jumped in to clear it up, and as Daneyko and I were separated and sent to the box, he looked at me and said, "Berard, that wasn't too smart. We are in the same division. I will get you again." I glanced over and saw he was smiling.

A few months later, I ran into Ken in New York City. I figured it would be rude to see him and not at least say hi, so I went over.

"Nice to see you, Berard," Daneyko said, shaking my hand.

"Good to see you, too," I said.

"I have to say, I've got a lot of respect for the fact you dropped the gloves against me," Daneyko said. "Not a lot of guys would do that."

I smiled sheepishly. "Mr. Daneyko," I said, "I didn't know it was you."

I lived with Bryan McCabe and Eric Fichaud that year in Muttontown, near our practice rink. We were all young players in the league, and we had a lot of fun living together. On nights when we didn't have a game, we usually went to the movies or headed to a local record store to add to our CD collection.

On weekends, the three of us often went out in Long Island, where the Islanders were a big deal. Everyone followed the team and knew who we were. We tried not to let it get to our heads, though. We'd heard stories from some of the older players about times when, if they were out too late or were in trouble at home, they'd call the local cop station and ask to stay the night in jail. They'd hide out there for the evening and leave quietly the next day. We always laughed at the stories, but we didn't want to be telling them ourselves. Needless to say, I grew up in a real hurry.

After home games on Saturday nights, we headed to a bar called Mulcahy's to grab a drink with the other guys on the team and listen to the live music. Bryan was a big music fan, and he loved to sing. Sometimes he would hop onstage with the bands and sing along to their songs. He could carry the tune, so the band never seemed to mind all that much. Moments like that were a welcome break from the stress of playing in the NHL.

I still kept close ties to my family, too. After I made the Islanders, my mom decided to get back at me for teasing her about her cooking when I was younger. She mailed two egg sandwiches to my house in Long Island for my birthday. The only problem was that I was on a long road trip that week. By the time I got back, the mailbox outside of the house reeked of egg sandwiches. I didn't even open the package—I could tell from the smell what they were. I chucked the sandwiches in the garbage and called my mom, and we had a good laugh.

I would have loved to have the sandwiches, too. Bryan, Eric, and I barely had anything in our fridge. None of us knew how to cook, so we always went out to eat. If we wanted something for breakfast on the way to the rink, we would stop at a coffee shop and grab something. There were a lot of single guys on the Islanders at the time, so most days, we'd have a team lunch after practice.

One of our go-to restaurants was a place called Vincent's. It was known around Long Island as one of the better Italian restaurants in the area. We stopped there before almost every home game for our pre-game meal. If we weren't there, we were eating at Ruth's Chris Steak House or the Barefoot Peddler.

Most of the time, the bill for our meals was reasonable. But during one road trip halfway through the season, the older guys decided it was time for the rookie dinner. Eric Fichaud and I were considered the rookies that year, and our initiation was taking the rest of the team out to dinner. We made a reservation at a high-end steak house in New York City. As we drove to dinner, Eric and I exchanged glances—the guys had healthy appetites, and we were on the hook for the bill. The guys talked a big game about all of the lobster they were going order, but thankfully, they were quite reasonable that night. Eric and I each had to shell out a few thousand dollars, but we didn't mind—we were a band of brothers.

When I played for the Islanders, you could go out every night and nobody would ever know. When we were home, you just had to go into New York City and nobody would ever find out that you had gone out.

On the road, whenever we got back to the hotel after a game, we a had a ten-minute rule. You had ten minutes to put your stuff in the room and get ready to go out. Each time, without fail, when I went back down to the lobby, there would be at least ten to twelve guys there, ready to go out and have a drink.

We were always back at the hotel by our eleven o'clock curfew, and we were always up in the morning for the game-day skate. It helped that we were young, and we knew the next morning that we could sweat out whatever we put in the night before. We had a term for it—"playing guilty." If you went out too late the night before, you played harder to make up for it. It was a good way of keeping each other honest and accountable. No one minded if guys went out and had a good time, just as long as they were ready to put the team first when we hit the ice.

•   •   •

In October 1996, I received my first signing bonus check with the Islanders. It was for $75,000, and as soon as I got it, I drove the check over to my parents' place. My parents freaked out when they saw it. The two of them had raised six kids on $40,000 a year. The idea that I was holding almost twice their yearly income in my hand was foreign to us all.

"It's amazing, Bryan. Just don't put all your eggs in one basket," my mom joked.

"Congratulations," my dad said, slapping me on the back. "Although the amount of taxes they're taking off is criminal."

It was a lot of money for my parents, let alone a young kid like me. Right away, though, I realized that I had to be smart with my money. I'd heard some of the horror stories of guys burning through their money too fast and having nothing left to show for their career years later. I didn't want to be like them—I wanted to be smart with my money.

Thankfully, I didn't have expensive tastes. The only luxury item that could tempt me was a car—I was the son of a mechanic, after all. But that could wait. For now, I knew I had to set myself up for the future.

I'd known for a while how important it was to make sure I was thinking about the future. Toward the end of my second year in the OHL, I was approached by a sports card company called Signature Rookies. The company wanted to use my photos in some special cards they were producing. I was cautious at first, but then they told me that they would pay me six figures as part of the deal.

I couldn't say no. I planned to use the money to help my parents pay a bunch of their outstanding bills. My dad's garage was still going through a downturn at the time, and I knew my family could use the help. This seemed like the best way to give them what they needed and give back to my parents, who had sacrificed so much for me.

I deposited my first check from Signature Rookies after signing the deal with them. The check cleared, and I could see the funds in my account. But two days later, the money was gone—the check had bounced. The company cut another check, which was cleared by the bank.

But that first payment was all I ever saw from the company. It ended up going bankrupt, and I—along with a bunch of other players—was left high and dry.

I knew I was never going to see the money I was owed. I was disappointed in myself for not handling the deal better, and I was angry at the company. All I wanted was to help my family—that was the only reason I'd agreed to the deal in the first place—and now I couldn't even do that.

Given that early lesson I'd learned, like a lot of guys in the NHL, I decided to rely on a financial advisor to take care of my money while I was busy playing hockey. And I had a guy in mind: Phil Kenner.

Phil had started trying to recruit me while I was still playing junior hockey. He was a financial advisor at State Street in Boston, where he worked with former Bruins player, the great Derek Sanderson. Derek would go out with Phil Kenner and recruit hockey players to become clients.

During one of their first recruiting trips, Derek and Phil came by my parents' house. We'd had some preliminary conversations with them over the phone, and we felt it was time to finally meet face-to-face. We all knew Derek Sanderson and his story—he had been an all-star with the Bruins who had fallen on hard times after he was done playing, and he ended up losing everything. Phil had played a little hockey, too, so we spent the first few minutes bonding over shared experiences. Phil had a nice way about him—I hit it off with him right away. The whole meeting felt like the type of recruiting trips from hockey coaches that we'd sat through when I was younger.

After Derek and Phil left, I was feeling good, and I was ready to trust Phil and Derek with my savings. But first, I wanted to talk with my parents about it.

"What did you think?" I asked them.

"I don't know much about investing," my dad said. "All I know is you need a professional of some sort to help you."

I looked at my mom. Her arms were crossed and she had a frown plastered across her face.

"What do you think, Mom?" I asked. I knew that look, though.

"There's something about that Phil guy I don't trust," she said. "Something doesn't seem right."

She couldn't put her finger on it, and nothing I said made her feel better. Eventually, I promised that I would only invest half of my savings with Phil. The other half I would invest with an advisor from Rhode

Island we knew, Peter McGeough. Peter knew how life in the NHL worked, too—he'd been drafted by the Islanders, but he'd suffered a bad back injury before he had a chance to play in the big leagues.

That seemed to make my mom happy. I headed back to Long Island feeling like I was on cloud nine. I had made the mature decision to set myself up for the future. Now it was time to focus on the present.

•　　•　•　　•

Throughout my rookie season, I was learning that, if I was going to give the team my all, I was going to have to improve a few areas of my game.

When I broke in to the NHL, I was an offensive defenseman. When I was playing in Rhode Island, my skating always made up for my lack of skills in other areas. I was able to close gaps quickly or get ahead of forwards breaking into our zone, so I never paid enough attention to the nuances of defensive positioning and angling—the basics that I should have mastered by the time I was twelve or thirteen years old.

We finished second to last in our conference that season. It was a rebuilding year for us, and although we had a losing record, we had grown closer as a team, and we were optimistic about what we might be able to accomplish the next season.

When the season ended, I received some humbling news: I'd been nominated for the Calder Trophy as the NHL's rookie of the year. Ginger Killian, the woman who ran the Islanders' PR department, called me to tell me that I had been nominated. Jarome Iginla of the Calgary Flames and Jim Campbell of the St. Louis Blues were the other nominees. When I heard that, I was amazed to be placed in such talented company.

I flew to Toronto after the season for the awards ceremony. I was looking forward to the event, and I figured it would be low stress. I was so sure that Jarome Iginla was going to win the Calder that I didn't prepare a speech. Okay, I also procrastinated—I had a severe anxiety about speaking in front of large groups, and I figured that if I didn't prepare, I didn't have to think about how embarrassing and awkward giving a speech in front of people might be.

When they announced the candidates for the Calder, I sat uncomfortably in my seat. Then, I heard the announcer: "And the winner of the 1997 Calder Trophy is . . . Bryan Berard."

I immediately went numb. The first thing I thought was, *Don't screw up your speech.*

My speech was a total disaster. I got up onstage, and I looked like a deer in the headlights. I read my opening lines, then looked up from my cards to the crowd. The moment I looked up, my mind went completely blank. Through the bright stage lights, I could just barely make out everyone in the audience staring back at me, waiting for me to say something. But my tongue wouldn't work. I blurted out a few more thank-yous and then quickly walked off the stage, the back of my neck getting more and more red.

Everyone had a good laugh at my expense that night. My family was chirping me worse than anyone.

"Make sure you don't quit hockey, because you don't have a career as a politician ahead," my brother Greg joked.

When the shock wore off, the awe set in. I was humbled by the company I was placed in. Later that night, I posed for a photo with Brian Leetch, who had just won the Norris Trophy as the league's best defenseman. I looked up to Brian—he was a fellow American who showed me what an elite defenseman could do on both ends of the rink.

As I looked at the trophy in my hands, I knew it was an immense honor, but it was more than a recognition of what I'd done—it was a symbol of what I still had to do.

5

DREAMING OF OLYMPIC GOLD

AFTER WINNING THE CALDER TROPHY, I WAS CONVINCED I'D BE PLAYING FOR the Islanders for years. The day after the awards ceremony, Mike Milbury called me to tell me that everyone on the Islanders was proud that I had won, and that it would give the fans hope for the future. I was touched, and I wanted nothing more than to make that hope of future success a reality.

But nothing is guaranteed in life or in hockey, and our work was set out for us the next season. The summer after my rookie year, I lived in Newport, Rhode Island, and trained at a place called Northeast Sports Training in nearby Warwick. Brian Boucher, mutual friend Matt Jarrett, and I rented a place together in Newport so we could spend as much time training as possible without distraction.

Our training camp that September was in Lake Placid, New York. We went through the usual rounds of cuts, and then, once he'd finalized the team for the season, Milbury staged a mini-Olympics for the guys on the final roster as a team-building exercise.

One of my favorite parts was when we got to race down the Olympic bobsled run in Lake Placid. It was the end of summer, so the bobsled had wheels on it instead of runners on the ice, but you could still pick up some serious speed.

Afterward, we split up into two-man teams for canoe races on the lake. Claude Lapointe and Roberto Luongo were in the same canoe, and when it was their turn to race, they went all out. They were flying along when suddenly their canoe started to tip over. They flailed their paddles, trying to keep it steady, but it just made things worse and suddenly, the boat flipped over and both guys were in the water.

The rest of us on land were howling with laughter, but suddenly, somebody shouted, "Luongo can't swim!"

That got us moving in a hurry. The canoes were in fairly shallow water close to shore, so a bunch of us sprinted into the water to grab Luongo and get him to safety.

"Save the rookie!" Milbury kept yelling from the shore. Thankfully, Luongo was hanging on to the capsized canoe, and we were able to get him out of there safely. We called an end to the canoe races after that.

After the fun of training camp was over, we got down to work. The coaches' expectation of me in my second season was clear: I had to fine-tune my decision-making on the ice. They started called me the "Riverboat Gambler" for how often I took chances with the puck.

"You made enough good decisions to win the Calder," Milbury told me. "But that's not enough to win a Cup. You can't always be jumping up in the play recklessly. You need to pick your spots better."

I knew the coaching staff was just trying to help me become a better player and help the team improve. But breaking those old habits and going against my competitive nature was hard. If we fell behind, I would pinch in the offensive zone and try to turn the momentum of the game around. I hated the thought of sitting back and watching us lose 5–2.

"What's the difference if we lose six to two or five to two?" I'd argue. "But if we take a chance and turn it around, we might have the momentum to make a comeback." My arguments always fell on deaf ears, though.

My whole second year in the NHL was a struggle. Even though my offensive numbers were almost identical to my rookie year, my plus-minus was bad, showing that I was on the ice for more goals against than scoring chances I was creating. The whole team struggled that year and the coaching staff were trying everything to turn us around. I always found I played my best defense when I was playing my best offense.

When I was on my game offensively, that meant I was up in the play and making things happen. When that happened, I typically had good gap control on the back end, too. Any time that I tried to hang back and be more careful defensively, though, I felt like I was being caught flat-footed. I would often overthink things and end up making a bad play.

At the beginning of my second season with the Islanders, Milbury hired six different assistant coaches in hopes of turning the team around. One of them, Bill Stewart, in particular was an immense help to me. Bill worked with me on a ton of drills throughout the season. He'd put me through the paces on the ice, and we'd review video together after practices so that I could improve my hockey IQ. Working with Bill, I got better at knowing when to take chances offensively and when I needed to play things safe.

We lost forty-one games that year. With each loss, my confidence slipped a little more and I became more likely to take risks.

Partway through the season, my agent, Tom, called me. He said that he'd had a weird conversation with Mike.

"Mike said something weird," Tom told me. "He said, 'I'm going to break him.'"

"What does that mean?" I asked.

"Good question," Tom said. "But we need to clear the air."

Mike, Tom, and I met at the hotel next to Nassau Coliseum on Long Island and had breakfast. Tom didn't beat around the bush.

"Mike, you said you were going to break Bryan. What do you mean by that?" Tom asked.

Of course, Mike denied he'd said anything of the sort. Tom and I knew I was far from a perfect player at that point in my career. Tom liked to say that I was a raw piece of clay that needed to be molded. And I recognized that Mike was going through a tough time in his life. Some days, he was totally fine and a decent guy. But he could become a totally different person the next day.

Looking back, I regret how our relationship was playing out. We had a love-hate relationship, but I was young and headstrong, and I reacted that way. Any time I make a mistake or made a bad decision on the ice, Mike would get irate and start yelling at me on the bench. I would tell him to "fuck off" during a game, and he would bench me for the next period. I probably should have kept stuff like that behind closed doors. And deep down, I knew that the coach's word ruled. I had to be a part of the solution for the team; otherwise I was just being part of the problem.

Part of the challenge was that Mike was still the general manager of the team. He had the ultimate say over who stayed and who got traded. And toward the end of my second year, it seemed that Milbury was trading everyone. He shipped out Bryan McCabe and Todd Bertuzzi to the Vancouver Canucks for Trevor Linden. Shortly after, people started to whisper that I was next.

Despite my battles with Milbury, I never thought there was any risk of my playing anywhere but Long Island. I figured we would butt heads during a long career I'd have with the Islanders. I even talked to Milbury about it, and he kept saying to me, "I'm not going to trade you." I figured as I gained more experience and my decision-making improved, Milbury would calm down and forget about the idea of trading me. I just needed to mature a bit. And luckily, I was about to have a chance to do exactly that.

•   •   •

The highest point of my second pro season had nothing to do with the NHL. Toward the end of 1997, I was named to Team USA for the 1998 Winter Olympics in Nagano, Japan.

I almost thought it was a joke when I heard the news. Just two years earlier, before my first training camp with the Islanders, I had watched every second of the World Cup of Hockey. Team USA beat Canada in the gold-medal game that year, and the tournament had shown me how inspiring it could be to play under your country's flag. I felt the hair on the back of my arms stand up as I thought about having the chance to play in a tournament like that.

Lou Lamoriello, then the general manager of the New Jersey Devils, was also the general manager of the American Olympic team that year. We were in the same division as the Devils, so we played them often, giving Lou a good look at my playing style in the lead-up to the Olympics.

When I saw the roster, I was honored that USA Hockey allowed me to be a part of the incredible group of players they'd assembled. The defensive corps was filled with all-stars like Brian Leetch and Chris Chelios, as well as the Hatcher brothers, Kevin and Derian. And up front, there was a stacked forward lineup that included guys like Bill Guerin and Tony Amonte. I was in heaven. For an American kid who grew up watching all those guys play in the NHL, the thought of pulling on the red, white, and blue jersey and standing beside them on the ice as their teammate—as their equal—was surreal.

I was just twenty years old at the time. As one of the youngest guys on the team, I wondered how I was going to fit in with the rest, which was made up of players who had a ton of NHL and international experience. I told myself that I would listen more than I would talk, and that I'd watch closely how the veterans behaved and take my cues from them.

We all met in San Francisco, where we boarded the Team USA charter jet. We made a quick fuel stop in Anchorage, Alaska (where it was a complete white-out when we landed), and then we flew straight to Nagano.

The moment the plane took off, I was relieved to see that the dynamic on the plane wasn't much different from what I usually saw on the team bus. Some guys settled in for naps, a few pulled on headphones and cracked open a book, and a bunch of us—including Tony Amonte, Jeremy Roenick, Keith Tkachuk, and Mike Modano—gathered in the back for a poker game. I looked around the table at the other guys and thought, *I wonder how seriously these guys take their cards?*

The answer was incredibly seriously. I shouldn't have been surprised—I'd found that most guys from the Boston area enjoyed their card games.

Over the next few hours, the other guys on the plane would wander back from time to time to see what was going on. At one point, Brian Leetch came back to watch the game, but it kept going for so long that he eventually left to go have a nap.

We were all in such a zone that we barely heard or noticed anyone else watching us. Finally, though, we heard an announcement come over the intercom.

"We're about to start our descent into Tokyo. Please take your seats and fasten your seat belts."

I looked at my watch and blinked a few times. We'd played for eighteen hours straight!

On the drive to the Olympic village, I was blown away at just how beautiful Nagano was. I had no idea what it would look like and when we arrived, it far exceeded my expectations. I laughed quietly to myself as I thought back to my first trip abroad to Berlin almost a decade before. A lot had changed since then, but in a lot of ways, I was still an eager-eyed kid who was excited to see a new part of the world.

The Olympic village looked like a big college campus. We were split into pairs for our rooming assignments. The rooms themselves looked like college dorms—each dorm had three bedrooms and two single beds in each room. I bunked with Keith Carney, one of the other defensemen on the team. Carney was a big guy—six feet, two inches tall and about 210 pounds—and he was from Providence, Rhode Island, so we got along well. Brian Leetch and Derian Hatcher were in another room, while our goalies—Mike Richter and John Vanbiesbrouck—were in the third.

As we were unpacking, Hatcher decided to take a break and watch some TV. A couple of minutes later, I heard a loud snap followed by a thump. I whipped around and saw Hatcher, a confused look on his face, sitting on the floor with a bunch of pieces of broken wood around him.

"What did you do?" I asked.

"Nothing," Hatcher said. "I was just sitting."

When we regrouped with the team, we found out the that the same thing happened to a few of the other big guys on the team, too. It turned out the furniture in the dorm rooms just wasn't built to handle the sheer size of some of the guys on our team. As we walked down the hallway of our dorm, we had to laugh at the piles of broken wood stacked outside so many of our doors.

What impressed me most, though, was the cafeteria they had set up for the athletes. Companies from all around the world had set up stalls where you could go get food. I was overwhelmed by the choice, but more than once, I was just too hungry and defaulted to McDonald's (athlete diets weren't as regimented back then).

We settled in that first day, and then the next morning, it was down to business. The tourist attractions of Nagano would have to wait—we had our sights set on an Olympic gold medal.

Me skating on the rink for the first time ever. It was the first of many times to come.

Apples don't fall far from the tree. My dad had poor sight in his right eye, so he cut a hole in the wire face mask of his helmet to help him see better.

The skating pond in our neighborhood was always busy during the winter, and I often headed there after school to hang out with my friends and play shinny. Here I'm in the red hat, skating with my dad and siblings.

My younger brother, Greg (*right*), and me, each of us wearing our new Woonsocket North Stars hockey gear.

Germany 1990
Hockey Friendship Tournament
Wally, Pam, Greg, Bethany, Uncle Greg

Sightseeing in Germany in 1990 with my mom and dad (*back row*), and my siblings Greg, Bethany, and Bruce (*front row, left to right*).

Our team was able to travel to the Friendship Tournament in Germany that year thanks to the generosity of so many people in the Woonsocket community. We chiseled off pieces of the Berlin Wall behind us to bring home as souvenirs. I'm in the back row, fourth from the right. My brother Greg is in the red pants in the front row, and Brian Boucher is the fourth kid from the left in the back row (with his collar popped).

Ever since I was young, I'd dreamed of playing for Mount Saint Charles Academy, a Woonsocket-based school that also happened to be one of the best hockey academies in the United States.

WOONSOCKET NORTH STARS

This was one of the final years I played for the Woonsocket North Stars. Between my school season with Mount Saint Charles and my games with the Mass Bay Chiefs, there were only so many games I could fit in.

I joined the Detroit Junior Red Wings in 1994. There were some tough characters around the league that year, so things could sometimes get rough.

Playing with the Select-16 team in Quebec in 1994 was one of the first times I had the privilege to represent my country in a tournament.

During the 1994 CHL All-Star Challenge, my dad sat next to Walter Gretzky in the stands. I always wondered how my dad explained to him why I fought Terry Ryan during the game.

Being selected first overall in the 1995 NHL Draft was a dream come true.

The best part about draft day was that my family was there to celebrate with me.

Front row, left to right: My dad, Wally; my brother Bruce; my mom, Pam; my sister Beth; my sister-in-law, Cathy; me.

Back row, left to right: My brother Greg; my sister Linda; my brother-in-law, Terry; my brother Dave.

I first met Mike Milbury when I was considering where to play for junior. Years later, he was the one who brought me to the New York Islanders, where I would start my NHL career.

When I broke into the NHL, I was an offensive defenseman. I loved rushing the puck and covering the point on power plays. In my mind, the best defense was a good offense.

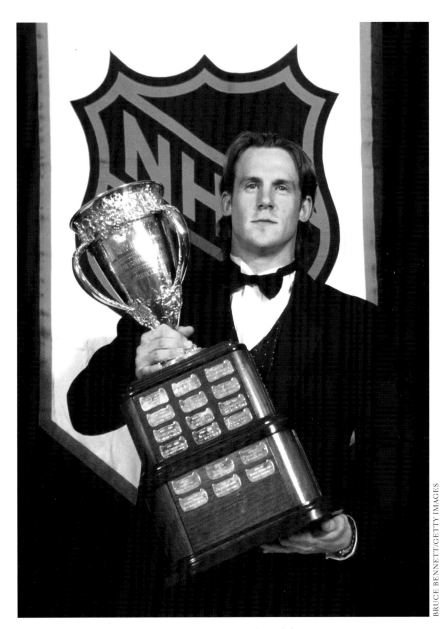

Winning the Calder Trophy as the NHL's rookie of the year in 1997 was an immense honor. Here I'm trying to forget how bad the speech I gave was and savor the moment.

When I went to the Nagano Olympics in 1998, I flew my parents and brother Bruce over, too. I was going to compete against the world's best players, and I wanted to do my family and my country proud.

The second I arrived in Toronto, I realized I'd won the hockey lottery. It was a great city filled with the most passionate fans I'd ever seen.

When Marian Hossa's stick accidentally clipped my eye, I immediately knew something was wrong. I tried to open my eye, and all I could see was darkness.

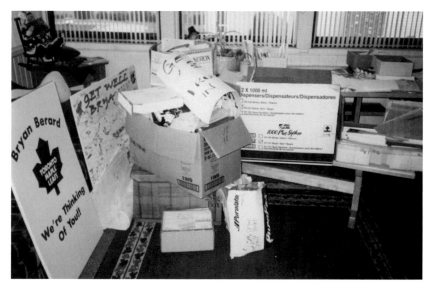

The outpouring of support from fans and well-wishers after my injury was over-whelming. I was grateful for each message, and every single one helped to give me hope during that difficult time.

Some of my favorite moments from my career were times like this, sitting around and sharing a drink, a meal, and a story with people like (*left to right*) Eric Fichaud, Brett Lindros, and Bryan McCabe, my teammates and roommate at the time. This is at the Barefoot Peddler in Long Island.

When I won the Bill Masterton Memorial Trophy in 2004, there was no way I could express the depth of my gratitude to everyone who helped me make it back to the NHL. It was a long journey, but I had never given up on my dream.

Shortly after we started filming *Battle of the Blades*, Wade Belak tragically died. We dedicated the show to him that season, and I did my best to raise as much money and awareness as I could for mental health.

My family has been my rock throughout my life. I wouldn't be where I am today without them.

At our first few practices, we were all still getting over the jet lag, but none of the guys held back. Toward the end of our first practice, Brett Hull skated over to me.

"Hey, kid, feed me some passes," he said. "I want to practice my one-timers."

I was excited to help Hully work on his one-timers. I got a bunch of pucks together and skated to the left point. Hull set up at the top of the circle on the right-hand side, and I started zipping passes to him. Each time, he unleashed a one-timer that ripped into the mesh in the top corner of the net.

After a few passes, I said, "Hully, how are those passes? Where do you like them?"

He laughed and said, "Look who you're passing to, kid—just put them anywhere you want!"

I howled. And it was true, I could pass the puck anywhere near Hull, and he would get the shot off. And my God, Brett Hull could shoot the puck.

Moments like that were fun, but I took my role seriously. I wanted to do my part and play up to the level of the guys around me. I tried to shadow Chelios and Leetch to see what I could learn from them. The lesson was simple: work harder than everyone else.

Chelios and Leetch were legends in the eyes of most hockey players. Back in the NHL, Leetch and I would often battle in front of the net or in the corner. After every whistle, we would give each other a tap on the shin pads before going back to our respective benches. He went about his work in a quiet manner, but he didn't have to say much—he commanded respect.

Both guys were machines, too. Chelios was often on the stationary bike . . . in the sauna. And Leetch started his workouts with a "light" warm-up of forty minutes on the bike. They were the first guys at the rink, and I saw how they were always working to get themselves ready for the next game. It wasn't just me who recognized their effort, either. When one of them spoke, the entire room listened.

I knew when we arrived in Nagano that I was going to be either the seventh or eighth defenseman and that I wouldn't be getting a lot of ice time. I was more than fine with that. Whatever time the coaching staff gave to me, I was determined to make the most of it.

I was pleasantly surprised, then, when our coach, Ron Wilson, decided to pair me with Brian Leetch on the first power play unit. I had watched Leetch and Sergei Zubov on the Rangers' power play plenty of times, and I had always been impressed by the way they could zip the puck back and forth. Now I could take what I'd seen and channel it myself, the same way I'd watched the older kids from the bench on the ponds in Rhode Island, waiting for my chance to hit the ice.

In our first game of the tournament, against Sweden, I saw the ice only when we had the man advantage. When we did get out on the power play, I was often cold because I'd been sitting so long, so I decided to keep my play simple. The entire time I was out there, I was looking to get the puck to Brian. He was so smooth with the puck and always made a perfect pass, so I figured it made sense to feed him the puck and let him go to work.

We lost that game 4–2, and afterward, I kept running through the game in my mind. I knew I hadn't played my best. So I went to Ron Wilson to talk about it.

"Ron, if I sit and get cold on the bench and only jump out for the power play, it will hurt the team," I said. "I'm more than happy to sit on the bench and only fill in if you need a seventh or eighth guy to grind down the clock. But I don't want to cost us opportunities to score."

"I appreciate your attitude," Ron said. "Let me think about it."

The next game, against Belarus, I took a back seat as the veterans went about their work. We won 5–2, but during the game, Tony Amonte got hurt. At the next practice, I was surprised to see my name listed at left wing on the fourth line, alongside Pat Lafontaine and Joel Otto. It had been a long time since I'd played forward, but if that's what the team needed, that's what I'd do.

We played a strong Canadian team for our final round-robin game. I knew how intense the rivalry was between Canada and the United States. I'd seen it going all the way back to the tournaments I'd played in as a teenager, and I was excited to relive it again at the highest level possible.

USA Hockey had beat Canada in the gold-medal game at the World Cup of Hockey in 1996, so the expectations were high heading into the game. Most of the guys on the Olympic team that year had been part of that gold medal–winning team, so if they were nervous, they sure didn't show it.

The Canadian team was a strong one that year, and they came at us from the very first whistle. We got an early power play, but we couldn't get one past Patrick Roy. Canada went up 1–0 late in the first, and in the intermission, we did our best to rally. But the onslaught continued in the second and then into the third. Brett Hull managed to score a goal with about five minutes left in the game, but when the buzzer went off, Canada came away with the 4–1 win.

We were disappointed, but we tried to put the game behind us and focus on the upcoming knockout round. Our record in the round robin meant we were pitted against the Czech Republic in the quarterfinals.

We knew the Czech team had some incredibly talented scorers, like Jaromir Jagr, and a good defense. But that wasn't what worried us. What worried us was one man: Dominik Hasek. The Czechs only allowed four goals against in the round robin, largely thanks to Hasek putting on a display of goaltending for the ages. He was in the kind of zone that you just don't see that often.

The mood before the quarterfinal game was more tense than it had been against Canada. We all knew what was riding on the game. Win, and we were one step closer to a medal. Lose, and we were headed home.

The first period was back and forth, as we threw everything we had at Hasek, looking for a break. He was standing on his head, and we wondered how long it would take to wear him down. But then, with just a few minutes left in the first period, Mike Modano ripped a shot past Hasek to give us the lead. As Modano cruised past the bench, high-fiving each of us, we felt a sense of relief, knowing we were on the board.

That relief was short-lived, though. The Czechs came out with a new energy in the second period, and they poured in three goals in six minutes to storm ahead.

We did everything we could to get back in the game, firing shot after shot. But Hasek was back on his game, stacking the pads and throwing himself across the net to stop everything. With less than a minute left in the game, we pulled the goalie, desperate for a goal. Instead, the Czechs fired the puck into our empty net, sealing the deal.

When the game ended, we had taken thirty-nine shots on net to the Czechs' nineteen, but it wasn't enough. Hasek had stolen the game again, and our Olympic dreams were done.

The next day, I barely spoke to anyone. The whole tournament felt like it had gone by in the blink of an eye, and we'd mustered only one win. *What could I have done better?* I wondered.

I did take some solace at the fact that USA Hockey brought home a medal. I grew up with Sarah DeCosta, who was the backup goalie for the women's team in Nagano. Sarah was my age, and when I was growing up, she was one of the best goalies in the entire state, man or woman. I played against her in high school—she was the starting goalie for the Toll Gate High School boys' hockey team—and she was incredibly talented.

Sarah and the women's hockey team went undefeated the entire tournament. I was so happy seeing my friend receive a gold medal around her neck. It didn't completely wipe away the disappointment I felt, but it helped.

Our last night in Nagano, we had a team dinner, and then we headed out to a karaoke bar. A lot of guys' wives were along for the trip, so it was a nice chance for us all to hang out outside the usual confines of the rink. When we got back to the Olympic Village, a bunch of us tried to let off some steam by playing pranks on each other. One guy soaked another's mattress in the shower and then put the mattress back on the bed. Another guy fired off a fire extinguisher into a teammate's room to wake him up. The pieces of the broken chairs that we'd left outside our rooms became projectiles that we flung at each other as we ran up and down the hallway. I was twenty years old, but we were all acting like dumb teenagers.

The next morning, we realized we'd gone too far. Chelios quietly took care of everything. He knew the whole incident was getting a lot of media attention, and being the captain that he was, he dealt with the problem. He took all the responsibility on his shoulders and when we got back to America, he paid the entire bill out of his own pocket.

Still, the press and USA Hockey were looking for someone to blame the fiasco on. I was on the team bus heading back to Tokyo for the flight home when a couple of officials from USA Hockey and NHL security grilled me about what happened.

"Who did this? Who was involved?" one asked.

"You won't play for Team USA again if you don't tell us," another added.

I looked them all dead in the eye and said, "I'm not saying anything." I refused to say anything more to them the rest of the trip. I half expected someone to circle back to me, but that seemed to be the end of it.

When I finally got back to North America, I was exhausted for days. Part of it was the jet lag, but it was also an emotional hangover. The Olympics experience had been amazing, and just being part of that team was a humbling experience. It was an honor to wear the Team USA jersey and to play with Hall of Famers like Leetch, Chelios, and Hull. But there had been a lot riding on the team's performance, and we hadn't lived up to that.

And now I was back in my apartment, and I had to immediately get back into the rhythm of the NHL grind. We were in another re-building season that year with the Islanders, and there was increasing uncertainty about what direction the team was headed. I tried to remember the lessons in leadership and hard work I'd learned while I was in Nagano and bring those back to Long Island with me, each and every day. But each day seemed to bring another loss, another fight with Milbury, another scolding from the coaching staff. I kept my chin up and did my best to be a good teammate, but there were days when my body and mind felt pulled in two different directions.

When the season ended, I tried to put the difficulties of the past year behind me. *Next year will be different,* I told myself. If only I'd known just how different it would be.

6

HELLO, TORONTO

THE DAY I FOUND OUT THAT I HAD BEEN TRADED FROM THE ISLANDERS, I heard about the deal from a Sher-Wood stick rep. It was January 9, 1999—almost three years to the day since I'd been traded from Ottawa to the Islanders. I was halfway through my third season in the league, and we were on the road in Montreal, getting ready to play the Canadiens. As soon as I got the call, I immediately rushed back to our team hotel.

When I got to the lobby, a group of guys from the team were there. "Where's Mike?" I asked.

"Up in his room," one of them said.

I raced up the stairs to Mike's room and knocked on his door.

"Come in," he said. When he saw it was me, he simply said, "It's too late. I traded you to Toronto for Felix Potvin."

I was silent. I never thought that I would be one of the guys Milbury would trade. As I left his room, I thought, *I've only been playing for the Islanders for two and a half years. What did I do wrong?*

But there was no time to dwell on my thoughts. I made my way back through the hotel to gather my things. I made a point to say goodbye to the trainers—they had taken good care of me, and I wanted them to know how much I appreciated their hard work—but otherwise, I didn't get much of a chance to say a long farewell to anyone. I didn't even go back to my condo on Long Island. I booked a flight from Montreal to Toronto. If there was change on the horizon, I figured I might as well jump right in.

• • •

The second I arrived in Toronto, I realized I'd won the hockey lottery. After just a couple of days in the city, listening to the sports radio and talking to people on the street, I could tell that I was in a great city filled with some of the most passionate hockey fans around.

The city had good reason to be excited about their team. The Leafs had an interesting mix of personalities and characters that year. There were seven Russian players, an incredible goaltending duo in Curtis Joseph and Glenn Healy, and a fierce competitiveness in guys like Tie Domi. And the undisputed leader was Mats Sundin, the captain and one of the most skilled players in the league at the time. It might have been an odd crew to bring together, but I got the sense right away that Mats was a respected leader. He reminded me of Leetch—quiet, but incredibly talented and competitive, and always leading by example.

I'd already played Toronto once that season when I was with the Islanders, so I knew they played a special style of hockey—they played a fast game with high-end skill and great goaltending, but they also had a ton of team toughness. When I joined the team, I realized that a lot of their success on the ice came from how tight-knit a crew they were off of it.

"Welcome to the team," Mats said, shaking my hand before my first practice with the team.

"Thanks," I said. "I'm really excited to be a part of the team."

Suddenly, a burst of laughter and rapid Russian echoed from the showers.

"That's just the Russian Mafia," Tie said, walking over and slapping me on the back. "Don't let them scare you."

"Are they good guys?" I asked.

Tie laughed. "*Da*," he said. "They are the best."

On February 13, 1999, a few weeks after I got to Toronto, we played the final game ever at Maple Leaf Gardens. It was an emotional night. The franchise was saying good-bye to the old-school, barn-style rink that had been its home for sixty-seven years. We played the Chicago Blackhawks, and when we got to our stalls before the game, we saw that we'd be wearing our Original Six sweaters that evening. Walking out through the tunnel to the ice, I could feel the crowd's energy rippling through the air. We could feel the history of the place seeping out of every beam and brick.

Unfortunately, we lost to the Blackhawks 6–2 that night. Bob Probert scored the final goal in Maple Leaf Gardens. Still, when the game ended and the emotional postgame ceremony was over, there wasn't a dry eye in the house.

A week later, we were back in Toronto, this time for the first game in our new home, the Air Canada Centre. The new arena had the best of everything. The dressing room, the weight room, the training room, and the players' lounge were all brand-new and the best that money could buy. It was clear that this was going to be a new era for the franchise, and moving into the new rink changed the mentality of it.

The guys on the team picked up on the energy. Every day, I woke up and I couldn't wait to get to the rink. We used to howl listening to Glenn Healy and Tie Domi tease each other every day. They'd kick things off and other guys would join in, and before you knew it, you felt like you were in a comedy club while you put on your gear before practice.

I'd only been in the league a few years, but I already knew that nothing was sacred in the locker room. You had to learn how to laugh not only at each other, but also at yourself. The guys all picked on my Rhode Island accent, but I didn't mind—it made me feel like I was back in my OHL days.

We often made fun of the Russian Mafia for sneaking cigarettes between periods. Not all of them smoked, but the ones who did (and the Canadians who joined them) would head to the laundry room between periods and have a quick butt standing next to the washer and dryer. They were always considerate of the rest of us, though—they'd blow their smoke into the dryer so that none of us smelled it.

One smell we couldn't avoid, though, was that of coach Pat Quinn's cigars. He would often puff on a stogie between periods while he was thinking about what to do the next period.

Pat Quinn knew what we had to work with, and he didn't try to complicate things. He just opened the door to the bench and let us play a run-and-gun-style game.

I appreciated the freedom. I liked old-school hockey, and Pat was as old-school as they come. While other teams were overcoached and played the trap most of the time, Pat was the complete opposite. We would jump over the boards and play high-tempo hockey. And if somebody wanted to mix it up, Tie and the boys were more than happy to drop the gloves. Pat was hard on us when he needed to be. Our practices were never more than forty-five minutes to an hour, but he worked us hard the entire time. He knew when to pound his big Irish fist on the water cooler or the whiteboard and get us fired up—whenever he pulled that move, the guys knew it was time to shut up and get serious. But most nights, once the game was on, he trusted us to go out there and just play. If he had something to teach us, he did it the next day on video and in practice.

I joined the power-play unit shortly after arriving in Toronto, and that was when I got to let loose. Tomas Kaberle was the playmaker on the power play, so my job was to help rush the puck into the other team's zone and set up the play for everyone else. Mats and I quickly worked out a play where we worked together to gain the zone. My go-to move was to carry the puck out of our end and then put the brakes on in the neutral zone. I'd hit Mats with a pass as he trailed the play. Mats would have a good head of stream at that point, and as he took my pass, he'd blow right by the other team's defense as they stood still around their blue line.

Playing that way was a bit of a luxury, of course. We couldn't have done it successfully without CuJo in net, ready to save the day at any time. Curtis Joseph was a defenseman's dream as a goalie. Especially an offensive defenseman, which I was. I often took chances in the offensive zone, looking for a break that could lead to a scoring chance for us. Sometimes, though, taking risks like that meant I was caught in a bad position, which led to a two-on-one, or even a breakaway, for the other team.

When that happened, CuJo would almost always make a big save to bail me out. He was excellent at reading players and guessing what they were going to do.

"Great save, CuJo," I'd say whenever that happened, tapping his pads. "You just saved my ass."

He'd just smile and say, "That's why they pay me the big money, B. Besides, I like making the big save."

CuJo liked a lot of shots on goal. He loved the action, and the more shots he faced, the better he played. Off the ice, he was the nicest guy you could imagine. But between the pipes, he was an athletic, aggressive goalie with wicked reflexes. And he was the best when it came to communicating with his defensemen. He told us exactly where he wanted us in the defensive zone.

Most of the time, that boiled down to one thing: get out of the way. Curtis liked to see the puck at all times—he didn't want us blocking shots. If we were killing a penalty or there was a battle in front of the net, CuJo would be screaming at me and the rest of the defensemen to get out of his way so he could see the shot.

That was usually for the best. When I played, there were only a few guys in the league who specialized in blocking shots. Luckily, one of them was my teammate, Danny Markov.

Markov was totally fearless when it came to blocking shots; he just didn't care if he got it and where the puck hit him. He knew how much it hurt to block a slap shot from up close, and still, he kept doing it, game after game.

One night, we were in Ottawa, and we were trying to kill off a five-on-three. Ottawa passed the puck back to the point, and their defenseman teed up a slap shot. Markov didn't hesitate and went down on one knee to block the shot. The defenseman leaned into his shot, and we watched as the puck slammed straight into Markov's face.

Thankfully, the puck was wobbling a bit, so it was flat when it hit him. Still, we could hear the wet slap as it struck his cheek.

The second the puck hit Markov's face, the refs blew the play dead, assuming he'd be injured. But Danny didn't go down. Instead, he skated toward the Ottawa bench and started chirping their bench the whole way in Russian. We asked the rest of the Russian players what he said, and they never did tell us. The Sens' players looked at him like he was nuts. Then again, so did we.

We all knew that Danny was hurt—his face was already swelling up as he skated back to our bench. It was funny and alarming at the same time. *That is some kind of pain threshold*, I thought as Danny sat on the bench and slapped an ice pack against his cheek.

They didn't call them the "Russian Mafia" for nothing.

•　•　•

I was a young defenseman when I arrived in Toronto, and I still had a lot to learn about the finer points of playing the position in the NHL. I was making bad decisions here and there, despite my best efforts to always make the smart play.

Whenever I messed up, Pat Quinn never said anything to me on the bench during the game. The next day, though, he would either pull me into the coach's office or talk to me on the ice in practice. If he called me into the office, I knew it was bad—Pat never gave you shit in front of everyone; he never wanted to embarrass any of us. I appreciated that. To be disrespected in front of your teammates by a coach is a horrible feeling.

I had quickly discovered that Pat Quinn knew everything that was going on in Toronto with his players.

One night, I stayed out until closing time, just after two in the morning. I went home, got some sleep, and made sure I was at the rink first thing the next morning. I was sitting in the players' lounge, watching TV and waiting for the other guys to arrive, when Pat walked by. He looked at me and said, "Berard, I hear you had your dancing shoes on last night." He grinned and walked on. *He must have spies everywhere*, I thought incredulously.

Pat always knew when we went out. He didn't care, though, just as long as we came to the rink to work and win. We didn't abuse Pat's trust. We all took great pride in being professionals, and we new when it was time to work. Of course, it helped that we were winning each night.

We played well the rest of the season, both at home and on the road. Whenever we were away from Toronto, my roommate was Steve Thomas. He was easy to room with, except for one bad habit. Each night, before bed, Steve liked to have a couple of cigarettes. It reminded me of my mom, who did the same thing. In both cases, I hated it. But I was a young player and Steve was a grizzled veteran, so I didn't say anything. I'd be lying in bed, and when I saw Steve go to light up a cigarette, I'd pull the sheets up to my nose to hide from the smell. The first time I did it, Steve looked at me like I was crazy, but he kept on smoking. He was a veteran, and I wasn't going to tell him anything.

I played thirty-eight games with the Leafs after my trade, and it felt like we got better every game. Before I knew it, the playoffs were on us.

Our first series was against the Philadelphia Flyers. It was my first experience with playoffs in the NHL, and I couldn't have asked for a better atmosphere. The fans of the Maple Leafs were die-hards. They could be hard on you if you weren't giving everything you had, but they were always respectful. When we headed into our playoff run in the spring of 1999, it was like the entire city was cheering us on.

On the day of our first game, I was filled with a nervous energy all day long. I didn't mind, though—I always played best when I had some nerves before the start of the game. It gave me an edge. Everything seemed a little clearer and sharper, as though my senses were on red alert.

The rest of the guys seemed to feel the same, but we fell short in our first game, losing 3–0 at home. It was an ugly game, and we didn't feel good about it afterward, and in the locker room after, we told ourselves we had to step it up in our next game.

But we had trouble scoring in the second game, too. The Flyers' goalie, John Vanbiesbrouck, was stopping everything we could throw at him. With less than two minutes left in the third period, we were still down 1–0. That's when I spotted my roommate, Steve Thomas, streaking through the neutral zone. I hit him with a pass, and Stumpy did the rest. He went tearing down the right wing and threw a backhand shot on net that slipped under the goalie's arm. His tying goal got the Air Canada Centre rocking. I could feel the cheers of the crowd reverberating through my body as we mobbed Steve in celebration.

I didn't think it could get any louder in the arena, but then, with less than a minute to go, Sergei Berezin carried the puck behind the Flyers' net. He wrapped around the net and threw the puck into the traffic in front. Sundin came down the left wing and the puck rolled out in front of him. He snapped the puck toward the net on his back-hand, and it beat Vanbiesbrouck over his shoulder.

We won the following game to pull ahead in the series. The Flyers tied it up after that, and then, in the crucial game 5, we pulled out an overtime win. That seemed to take the wind out of the Flyers' sails, and CuJo sealed the deal with a shutout in game 6 to give us the series win.

We immediately turned our attention to the semifinal series. Up next was the Pittsburgh Penguins. We fell behind two games to one in the series. Game 4 was back and forth, and Pittsburgh tied it up halfway through the third period. Only a couple of minutes into over-time, though, Sergei Berezin buried a loose puck that snuck behind the Penguins' goalie. We were headed back to Toronto with the series all tied up.

We won game 5 handily to take a stranglehold on the series. But in game 6, the Penguins came back with a vengeance. They stormed out to a 2–0 lead in the first period, but we clawed back to take the lead the next period. The Penguins tied it up 3–3, and we were in a deadlock the rest of the game. It seemed that if we were going to keep moving ahead in the playoffs, it was going to be in one overtime period after another.

This time, Garry Valk played the role of the hero. Yanic Perrault won a face-off in the Penguins' zone and we fired the puck on net. Tom Barrasso, the Penguins' goalie, couldn't quite control the re-bound. He was way out of his crease, and Garry stormed the net. The Penguins' defense tried to collapse on the puck, but Garry, as he was being knocked to the ice, shoveled the rebound home.

The moment we saw the puck hit the back of the net, we all poured off the bench and raced to celebrate with Garry in the corner. We were going to the conference finals—just four more wins, and the Stanley Cup would be within our sights.

That sort of forward thinking was our undoing, though. Before we could get to the Stanley Cup Finals, we had to get through the Buffalo Sabres. Which meant we had to get past Dominik Hasek.

We thought we caught a break when we found out that Hasek was going to be out with an injury for at least the first two games of the series. You might score a couple of goals against Hasek, but once he decided to shut you down, he shut you down, and it was over. With him out of the lineup, we saw a chance to get an early jump on Buffalo. But their backup, Dwayne Roloson, was equal to the task, and Buffalo won the first game 5–4. We managed to win the second game, but then Hasek was back. And just like in Nagano, it seemed there was no beating him. We only managed two goals each of our last three games in the series, which Buffalo won, setting them up for a Stanley Cup Final showdown against the Dallas Stars.

The room was silent as we put away our gear following the final loss. We all felt like we had choked and that we had looked past Buffalo. We'd been looking ahead to a match-up against Dallas and not thinking enough about what was right in front of us. All year, we'd felt like we had a great chance to get to the Cup final. We really felt that we had a team that could go all the way. Coming so close, only to fall short, stung badly. I hoped that next time the outcome would be different. More than that, though, I hoped there would be a next time.

•   •   •

After that 1998–99 season, Tom negotiated a two-year contract for me with the Leafs' assistant GM, Bill Watters. I was so excited to be locked in with the Leafs. I felt as though I was in a place where I could grow and learn, and where we had a chance to go all the way. It was exactly the sort of competitive atmosphere I'd been looking for, and I was so happy that I would get to keep living in Toronto.

After the disappointment of losing to the Sabres in the conference final the year before, I was determined to be even better the next season. Pat Quinn had made some moves to change up how we played— I got the sense that he wasn't convinced our run-and-gun style was sustainable in the long run. But the core pieces and veteran players were all there. We got off to a solid start and looked like a team ready to repeat the previous year's playoff success.

Early that 1999–2000 season, there was a line-clearing brawl. I wasn't much of a fighter, but every guy paired up with someone else. When I looked at who I was tangled up with, I felt a pit open up in my stomach. It was Craig Berube. Berube was renowned throughout the league as a tough enforcer, and he was way out of my weight class. *Buckle up*, I thought.

Berube hit me two or three times in the head. I was trying to throw a few jabs back, but he could have killed me if he wanted to. Thankfully, he seemed to take pity on me. He paused before one punch and said, "Just hang on, and we'll make it look good the rest of the way."

I didn't have much need to fight during the season because playing for the Leafs meant playing with Tie Domi. And no one was tougher than Tie.

I used to tease Tie a lot, especially in the weight room.

"Hey, Tie, how do you manage to hold the bar with such small hands?" I asked.

He laughed, and then he reached out, lightning-quick, and got me in a headlock. And once Tie grabbed you, it was over—he was so strong, there was no getting away from him.

"You want to see what these small hands can do?" he'd ask with a grin before releasing me.

"I'm just glad you're on my side," I said with a laugh.

Every single time that I fought in the NHL, I was exhausted afterward. I would be ruined for the rest of the period. I was happy not to fight, and instead to concentrate on playing my game and let the experts take care of it.

I mentioned to Tie how tired I got whenever I did fight. He grinned—he'd heard the same thing before.

"A lot of guys forget how to breathe properly during a fight," Tie explained. "Guys get so worked up that they hold their breath. If you don't want to get tired during a fight, take your time and breathe."

"Easier said than done," I said with a laugh. But I tried to remember Tie's trick the next time I dropped the gloves.

In November 1999, the Flyers were in Toronto to play us for a classic *Hockey Night in Canada* special. Brian Boucher had recently been called up the Flyers, and we made a point to meet up for dinner the night before and reminisce about Woonsocket and how far both of us had come.

The next night at the Air Canada Centre, though, all those pleasantries were behind us. Brian went into the game after the Flyers pulled Vanbiesbrouck, and I was determined to score on my best friend.

It was a chippy first period, and we were playing catch-up the entire time. Then, during the second period, all hell broke loose. The Flyers sent out their giants—Sandy McCarthy, Craig Berube, Luke Richardson, and Daymond Langkow. I looked across the ice and saw that Tie was lining up for the face-off. All four Flyers seemed to have their attention focused on Tie. *They must have been pissed about something he did in the playoffs,* I thought.

A few seconds later, a line brawl broke out. Guys paired off and started throwing punches. We'd all seen it before, and we yelled encouragement at the guys on the ice.

But then things became a gong show. CuJo started racing down the center of the ice. I looked at him, confused as to why he was leaving his net. But then I noticed a blur in the corner of my eye—it was Boucher, racing from the other end of the rink to square off against Curtis!

The two of them collided at center ice and started hanging on to each other, not sure what to do.

I started banging my stick on the boards, "Throw a punch or get off the ice, Brian!" I yelled, laughing my head off. Neither he nor Curtis knew how to fight. The brawl eventually fizzled, but after the game, we couldn't stop laughing at CuJo in the locker room.

As I looked around the room, I felt incredibly confident and at ease. I loved the city, I loved the team, and I loved my coach. I was ready to spend the rest of my career in Toronto. I didn't want anything to change. I wish I'd taken more time to appreciate that moment. Because just as I was hoping that everything would stay the same, my life and career were about to transform in ways I couldn't imagine.

7

EVERYTHING GOES BLACK

ON THE EVENING OF MARCH 11, 2000, JUST SIX DAYS AFTER MY TWENTY-third birthday, we were playing the Senators in Ottawa. I always enjoyed the away games in Ottawa. Ever since my trade to the Islanders, when I played in Ottawa, the crowd booed me any time I touched the puck. I never minded it. In fact, I enjoyed the intensity.

That night was an ordinary game like any other game I'd played in the NHL. I ate some pasta and chicken for my pregame meal, and I finished it off with a little bowl of ice cream, as I was always did. Then I took my typical afternoon nap.

After I woke up, I headed out the door, as I liked to get to the rink early. I picked up a coffee along the way, and I made it to the rink two and a half hours before the game. I settled into a quiet corner and put a heat pad on my lower back, trying to work out some of the lingering stiffness.

After I stretched, I taped up three new sticks, just like I did every game. Then I went through my typical mental visualization. I could see myself on the ice reading plays, working the point on the power play, and making breakout passes.

By the time I hit the ice for my warm-up, I was feeling good. I was ready to go to work.

We jumped out to an early lead, and Yanic Perrault scored a couple more goals early in the second to give us a comfortable lead. Ottawa was pressing, but we seemed to be in control. Things were clicking for us.

Partway through the game, we were on a four-on-four situation. The puck was in the corner, and I was covering Marian Hossa in front of our net. I read the play and saw that the Senators were going to force the puck into the slot. Mats Sundin picked off one of their passes, and my mind switched from shutdown defense to offense. I tracked the puck and shifted my weight forward, ready to jump into the play and head up the ice.

But just as I turned around, I saw Marian Hossa's stick coming straight for my face. He had tried to turn and one-time the pass that Sundin intercepted. He missed, but his follow-through carried his stick around.

I felt the toe of the stick connect with my right eye, and my world exploded in pain.

I threw down my stick and gloves and fell to the ice, crying out. I'm sure everyone, as they watched the scene unfold, assumed I was crying out in sheer agony. I was thrashing around the ice and kicking my legs. But it was less about the pain and more about the fear.

I tried opening my eyes, and everything was pitch black. All I could see through my left eye was a pool of blood gathering on the ice beneath my face. I had a panic attack. I honestly thought I'd lost my eye. I lay there, facedown, flailing my legs on the ice. I felt as though I'd left my body entirely. My brain wasn't working properly. All I could say was, "I can't see! I can't see!"

Through my cries, I heard CuJo's voice yelling for the trainers. When I heard the fear in his voice, I got even more scared.

My brain only registered the moment in fits and starts. Shortly after I hit the ice, our trainer, Chris Broadhurst—we called him "Broadway"—was by my side. He passed me a towel to hold under my eye, and within seconds, I could feel it was warm and sticky with my blood. I still couldn't see anything with my right eye, and I started to panic, taking in giant gulps of air. Broadway and Jonas Hoglund grabbed my shoulders and guided me off the ice as I glided along, doubled over in pain.

When I got off the ice, Broadway passed me into the care of another one of our trainers, Brent Smith. Brent hustled me to the dressing room, where two of the Senators' doctors were waiting for us.

The first thing the doctors did was sit me down and remove the towel to get a look at my eye. There was too much blood to get a clear look, so they gently sprayed eyewash on it to try to see what was wrong. As they examined my face, the doctors tried to keep a neutral expression. But Chris McAllister, one of my teammates, was a healthy scratch that night and he was standing behind the doctors. The look on his face when he saw my eye told me everything I needed to know—I was in serious trouble.

"We need to get you to a hospital," one of the doctors said.

I arrived at the hospital a few minutes later, shirtless and still wearing my hockey pants. Brent wouldn't leave my side the entire time, and he and the nurses guided me to what looked like a dentist's chair, where the emergency doctor examined me.

He looked at the eye for a minute and said, "We can't do this here."

When I heard that, I felt sick to my stomach. I ran to a garbage pail because I thought I was going to throw up. Then I had another panic attack. I broke out into cold sweats, and I felt the room spinning. My mind was racing a million miles an hour at this point.

The pain was bad—white-hot waves of pain that shot through my head and down my spine. But it was mixed with fear as terrible thoughts raced through my head—thoughts of being blind, of never playing in the NHL again, of never seeing the same again. But the fear remained much worse than the pain.

Before we left the room, the nurses gave me some medication to help reduce the pain and calm me down. It must have been powerful stuff, because I immediately blacked out.

The first surgery on my eye took eight hours. When I woke up, I was lying in a hospital bed. Brent was still there, sitting by my side, and I was relieved to see a familiar face.

"Brent, what's happening?" I asked. "What did the doctors say?"

Brent gave a small smile. "They'll be back in a little while. Just rest up," he said.

I could tell he was stalling. "Brent, what aren't you telling me?"

"The doctors think you should wait until your parents are here," he said. There was a snowstorm that night, and my parents were still trying to make their way to Ottawa.

That frustrated me. "I'm twenty-three years old. I can handle whatever they have to say. And I want to talk to the doctors. Right. Now."

The nurses brought me to a dark room, where they peeled the bandage off my eye. The eye was still completely swollen shut. But I looked in the mirror, and with my good eye, I could see that I had stitches above and below my right eye. That whole side of my face looked like a big piece of raw steak.

"What's wrong with my eye?" I asked the doctor as soon as they entered the room.

"You experienced what's called a pressure cut," the doctor explained patiently. "The stick ruptured the artery in your eye."

I felt my head spin. "That explains the blood," I said.

"Yes," the doctor continued. "The damage was severe. Your eye was basically cut in half."

"So you're saying my eyeball exploded?" I asked.

"In a sense, yes," the doctor said.

"Can you fix it?" I asked.

"That's what the surgery last night was intended to do. And we'll keep doing everything we can. But, Bryan, I have to warn you—I doubt you will ever see out of that eye again."

The doctor went on to explain the damage that I suffered. My cornea was cut in half. I lost my iris. I lost the gland the keeps pressure in your eye. And I suffered a lot of retina damage. Basically, it was about as bad an eye injury as you could imagine.

"Can't you just stitch it back up?" I asked. I could feel my heartbeat racing, and I tasted bile in my mouth.

"It's not that simple," the doctor said gently. "There's no easy way to say this, but if any tiny fragments of the stick or tape were dislodged, there's a chance that your eye could get infected. If your body rejects your right eye because of an infection, it could affect your left eye, too.

To stop that from happening, we may need to remove your right eye entirely."

I tried to speak, but my mouth had dried up completely. I had always taken for granted that my body would do what I wanted of it. I had been an athlete for so long that I'd never had reason to think otherwise. I couldn't wrap my head around the idea.

"I'd like to do a couple of tests," the doctor said. They covered my left eye, took out a flashlight, and shined it at my right eye. "Do you see anything?"

I squinted a bit and could make out a fuzzy impression of the doctor's light.

"I can see the light," I said, taking my hand down from over good eye. "It looks like I'm looking through a glass, but I can see some details."

The doctor's eyebrows shot up. "That's amazing," they said. "We weren't sure if you'd be able to see light at all, so this is a very good sign."

"So what do we do now?" I asked.

"For now, you have to rest. You've suffered a traumatic injury, and repairing it is going to take a long time. The best thing you can do is let your body recover."

I tried to take the doctor's advice, but my mind wouldn't slow down. I couldn't stop piecing the moment back together in my head. I didn't want to be alone with my thoughts.

Not long after that, Daniel Alfredsson, Wade Redden, and Marian Hossa of the Sens all came to see me in the hospital.

Hossa was crying as he entered the room. "I'm so sorry, Bryan," he said immediately.

I looked at him. "It's part of the game," I said. "It is okay. I am going to be okay. It is not your fault, Marian." I quickly started crying, too, and we talked quietly for a few minutes.

I meant what I said to Hossa. It was hockey—bad things could happen. The way that I was raised, I was taught to never ask, "Why me?" My parents had never asked why the business struggled, or why they had to put up with something. You focused on what made you happy and the positive things in life, and you gave thanks for that. Bad things could happen anytime, and there was no controlling that. But what you could control was how you reacted to those difficult moments, and how you overcame them.

Brent stayed by my side until my parents showed up, finally having made it through the snowstorm. They'd been getting phone calls from the Leafs staff with regular updates on my condition, and each time the phone rang, they were afraid to answer it. It took a lot to rattle my parents, but as they listened to the doctors fill them in on the extent of my injury and the next steps I faced, it looked like they'd each aged a great deal.

A few hours later, Steve Thomas showed up. The Leafs had gone back to Ottawa after the game, but Steve had hopped on the first flight back to Ottawa after they got home.

When Steve walked into the hospital room and saw me sitting beside my parents, he had tears in his eyes. Seeing that set me off, and the two of us had a good cry together.

He was my roommate and he was my friend. Steve Thomas was the kind of guy who would drop everything and fly to Ottawa to see you in the hospital. I will never be able to say thank you enough to Stumpy for doing that. I was at rock bottom, and seeing my veteran roommate standing beside me, crying with me, did as much to help me recover as the incredible work from my doctors did.

That night, when my parents went back to their hotel for a rest, they found a note slipped under their door.

> *Dear Mr. and Mrs. Berard, maybe a more experienced reporter than me would have tried to snap your picture this afternoon at the hospital.*
>
> *Maybe they would have tried to corner you on the way to the elevator. But I couldn't bring myself to do it. Maybe that makes me a lousy reporter.*
>
> *But when I saw you come in from the airport, you had your bags with you, and I saw the look in your eyes. I knew I couldn't live with myself if I had kept you away from your son for even a minute.*
>
> *I wish you luck, and I hope Bryan realizes that he has a lot of people pulling for him.*
>
> *Sometime, if you ever feel that you have time to talk; I would be grateful and honoured.*
>
> *Josh Rubin*
> Toronto Star

The note moved us deeply. The media had been anxious to get a quote from me or them about what happened, but we were all on lockdown. We just wanted to see each other, and we were still having difficulty processing what happened.

A few days later, I flew back to Toronto with my mom, my dad, and Brent. The next two weeks were critical, so my parents decided they would stay in Toronto with me. I had an apartment in the Yorkville neighborhood of the city, and they moved in with me for their stay. They helped me get back and forth to all the hospital visits, eye exams, and constant tests and checkups. I wanted to let them know that I was okay, that I could take care of myself—I didn't want them to worry. But I knew I needed the help, and I was grateful to have them close by.

I was under near-constant medical care to make sure that my brain wasn't rejecting my damaged eye. The doctors reiterated their decision—if they suspected that my brain and body were rejecting the bad eye, they would have to remove it immediately to protect me. In the meantime, the doctors continued to monitor and treat the eye in order to save whatever they could of it. It was a slew of constant checkups and exams, day in and day out.

I tried to remember my mom's lesson—"'Never' does not exist in our family's vocabulary"—and focus on the positives. I was overwhelmed and humbled by the support that I received. My family, teammates, and fans all sent me encouraging "get-well" messages, and I was immensely grateful for each and every one. Vince Carter even signed me a Raptors jersey to help cheer me up.

I took whatever bit of good news I could get, because there was plenty of bad news to go along with it. After the first surgery I'd had the night of the injury, I had a lot of bleeding in the back of my eye, and the doctors warned that the blood was toxic to the retina.

"We'll need to do another operation," one of the surgeons explained. "But we have to wait for the blood to clot before we can clear it out of your eye."

I went back to my parents' house in Rhode Island to recover. Each day, as the blood clotted in my eye, the light that I was able to see got dimmer and dimmer, to the point that I couldn't see any light whatsoever out of my right eye.

While we waited, we researched eye doctors across the continent. We were hoping to find someone who had facilities near my parents' place in Rhode Island. The doctors had warned me that, after the second surgery, I would have to lie facedown for weeks on end to allow my retina to heal. My parents had offered to keep looking after me during that time, so we needed somewhere close to home.

One name that kept coming up over and over was Dr. Stanley Chang, who operated out of Columbia-Presbyterian Hospital in New York City. He was at the top of a number of lists, so we reached out and scheduled the operation.

The day of my second surgery, Dr. Chang explained what he and his team would be doing.

"We have to go in and remove the blood from your eye," he said. "Then we can look at how best to repair your retina."

"Whatever it takes," I said.

"I know you want to play hockey again," Dr. Chang said.

"No," I corrected. "I want to play in the NHL again." The minimum vision required to play in the NHL was 20/400. A person with 20/400 vision was legally blind. My right eye wasn't even on the charts yet—I had a long way to go.

"Then let's see what we can do," Dr. Chang said.

Most people don't know this, but when you have eye surgery, you are not put out cold with general anesthesia. The doctors give you a local anesthetic so that you don't feel anything in the area they're working on, and you're kind of loopy. But you're awake and aware of what is going on.

I dozed off a few times over the next four hours. Each time I woke up, I could hear the doctors murmuring and the machines beeping. And every time that a little vision came back to my right eye during the procedure, I could actually see shadows of the doctors' instruments in my eye. It was the freakiest thing that I had ever been through.

Toward the end of the operation, one of the assistant surgeons was stitching up my eyeball. The anesthetic was beginning to wear off, and I was starting to feel the needle going into my eye as he stitched me up.

"Hey, Doc," I said. "I can feel that. And it's getting worse and worse."

"There are only a couple more stitches to go, hang in there," he said.

The last two stitches he put in, I could feel the needle going in and out of my eyeball while he did it. It was like someone was kicking me in the eye with steel-toed boots.

When I was wheeled out of the operating room, my parents were waiting, along with Ken Dryden, then the president of the Leafs. My mom told me afterward that Dryden sat with them through the whole operation—words could not even begin to describe how grateful our entire family was for the first-class treatment we received from every-one in the organization. They all tried to talk to me, but I could barely acknowledge them, though, because I was in so much pain.

When they finally got me to my recovery room, the pain was excruciating. They rolled me onto my side and stuck two needles in me to alleviate the pain. I slept in the hospital that night, and then the next day, my parents took me back to Rhode Island.

The next few weeks were a mix of boredom and fear. I had to remain as still as possible for as long as possible so that my retina would retain its shape and my eyeball could heal properly. That meant that I couldn't do anything after the surgery. I couldn't be active and walk around much, let alone work out. I had so much pent-up energy, and nowhere to direct it.

I was so thankful for the way my parents took care of me during that time. My mom had smoked her entire adult life. During the second surgery, though, she prayed that if the doctors saved my eye, she would quit smoking. When we got back to Rhode Island, she threw out her cigarettes.

Each day, my mom had to give me multiple eye drops, hour after hour. My mom hated eye injuries, and she was grouchy from quitting smoking, so she could never hit the target.

After a few days of getting the eye drops all over my forehead and cheeks, I said to my mom, "Ma, why don't you go back to smoking? You keep missing my eye."

The good news was that the drops were doing their job. But, just my luck, there was bad news to go along with it. Scar tissue kept building up over my eye. The doctors picked up on it in one of their regular exams. They were worried that, if the scar tissue continued to build up, it would eventually detach the retina again.

So, for the next three or four months, I went back to the hospital periodically for further operations. Each time, they would cut my eye open again to reattach the retina. Then they'd stitch up my eye again, and I'd head back to Rhode Island for more recovery. Eventually, we got the retina to heal and stay in place.

After each surgery, the doctors injected a silicon-based substance in my eye. After the injection, they brought me to a modified massage table, where I had to lie facedown for hours at a time to rest. The idea was that the silicon would flatten the retina and help it reattach to the rest of my eye. But sleeping like that was hard for me. I was typically a side sleeper, so I wasn't able to truly rest lying on my stomach with my eye full of silicon. Every time, the process left me exhausted and agitated.

And even after all of that, my eye still wasn't working properly. Instead of improving, the vision in my right eye was getting worse and worse. The blood was still clotting and interfering with the imagery traveling from my retina to my optic nerve. So it was back to the doctors' offices for more tests and treatments.

Despite all of the ongoing discomfort, fear, and setbacks, the hardest part with the healing process was the boredom. I just wanted to get back to my life again.

Slowly but surely, things got a little better. The doctors told me there was a two-year window in which my eye could regain a bit more of the vision it had lost. I knew I'd never get back what I had lost, but the thought of things getting better gave me some small measure of hope.

We eventually got to a point where Dr. Chang felt my retina had healed as much as it could. After my fourth surgery with Dr. Chang— my fifth out of seven surgeries overall—he gave me the green light to start being active again. It was late in 2000, and the weather was turning cold, but I was just happy to finally be outside and moving.

My younger brother was still at home, so we would play games to help improve my depth perception. We started by just tossing a baseball back and forth, but I felt that was a little risky, given my lack of depth perception. Then I switched to a football, which helped a lot— because it was bigger, it was easier to track, and I could gauge how far it was from me.

I would play catch with my brother for hours, and I found that just the simple act of throwing and watching the football helped improve my depth perception.

Even that simple action required focus, though. My vision was technically better, but my brain was used to having two good eyes, and the switch to just one hurt. My brain would sense me seeing something with my right eye and try to exercise it, but it didn't have enough vision in it to provide the information my brain needed. I had a pair of special Oakley glasses made that offered me some extra protection. But I still started closing my right eye anytime I had to read text, going over it with just my left eye.

After a few months, I graduated from light cardio to actually skating again. I wanted to test myself and see where I was at. So I called up Tim Army, the head coach at the Providence College hockey team, and asked if I could come out to skate with him. I wasn't ready to skate with the Leafs or any other NHL team. Tim had been one of my assistant coaches on the 1998 Olympic team. He was also a Rhode Island guy, and I knew him well. I trusted him to be honest and helpful.

The first time I stepped on the ice was a real challenge. It had less to do with my eye and more to do with the fact that I was so out of shape. I had gained at least twenty-five pounds while I was rehabbing my eye injury—I must have weighed close to 240 pounds at that point. Before my injury, skating and playing hockey felt so natural to me that I never thought about it. Now, I had to force the issue.

I did that for a few weeks, until the NCAA stepped in and ordered the team to stop allowing me to practice with them because I was a pro athlete. *Some pro athlete*, I thought. *I'm just a slow, out-of-shape, sluggish hockey player with one eye.*

But even in those dark moments, I never lost hope. Each day, no matter how bad things were when I was out in the world, I came home and had my family around me. When I was at rock bottom and wondering if I would lose my eye, they were with me every step of the way; willing me to get better. That was all that mattered, and it was enough to keep me going. I wasn't going to let this injury ruin my life. One way or another, I told myself, *I'm going to make it back to the NHL.*

8

THE BUMPY ROAD BACK

MISSED THE REST OF THE 1999–2000 SEASON BECAUSE OF MY INJURY, AND over the summer that followed, it was clear that, as much as I wanted to play in the NHL again, my return wasn't anywhere near in sight. In fact, after the injury, I was, for all intents and purposes, retired.

A few months after the injury, I received a check in the mail. It was for $6.3 million. I knew what it was—$6 million represented the payout from the personal insurance policy I had under my NHL Players' Association (NHLPA) agreement, and the rest were the payments from the NHL and NHLPA as part of their insurance policy for career-ending injuries.

I was twenty-three years old, and I was holding more money in my hand than I'd ever seen in my life. I could have retired right then and there and lived comfortably and taken care of my family. But instead of relief, I felt disappointment. That phrase—"career-ending"—bugged me. I wasn't ready to be done with the NHL. I had dreamed of playing in the NHL my entire life.

Still, I decided to start by playing things safe. After receiving the money, I called my insurance agent.

"If I make it back to the NHL, will I have to return this money?" I asked.

My insurance agent told me that I would definitely have to return the three hundred thousand dollars that I had received from the NHL and the NHLPA as part of their career-ending insurance policy. The bigger question was the $6 million I received as part of my disability policy. My insurance agent's understanding of the policy was that I would have to return the money. Years later, other lawyers who looked at the policy said that, because it was a disability policy, not a career-ending one, I should never have had to return the money. But at the time, I trusted my insurance agent's opinion, and I weighed my options accordingly.

I estimated I had close to $3 million in my savings when I hurt my eye. If there was a chance I never played hockey again, that meant that my days of earning a living in sports were over. That money might have to last me a long time.

•   •   •

After I was banned from practicing with the Providence College team, I went back to the rink at my old high school, Mount Saint Charles, in the quiet hours. Each day, when I could get the rink to myself, I would skate on my own. And each day, I got a little steadier on my feet and a little stronger. My eyesight wasn't improving, but it also wasn't getting any worse, so I considered that a small victory.

Eventually, I was confident enough to even start working with a personal trainer, a family friend from Rhode Island. After a few workouts, it was clear my body was still in rough shape, though.

"I need to kick-start my body somehow," I told the trainer.

Looking back, I should have turned down the offer that followed: an offer to take steroids as a way of speeding up my body's rebuilding process. But I was young, and frustrated, and I wanted nothing more than to get back to the one thing I knew best: hockey. I'd heard rumors of guys in the league taking performance-enhancing drugs. I wasn't looking for performance enhancement—I just wanted to get back to my normal.

The NHL wasn't testing for steroids at the time, nor did they have any rules against using them. I told myself I'd use the drugs to get strong enough to get back to where I was before the injury—*Just enough to speed up my recovery*, I thought—and then I would go back to my usual conditioning.

By the summer of 2001, after eight months of work in the gym and on the ice, I was skating a lot and really getting into good shape. At the same time that I was reworking my body into a healthy shape, I was trying to do the same for my mind.

That same summer, my agent, Tom, approached me about helping him in the office and learning what it takes to be an agent.

"I can show you the ropes, and we can see if you like it or not," he said cheerfully. I knew what Tom was trying to say: *Your playing days are over, and I want to help you find a way to make a living*.

I appreciated Tom's concern, and I'd be lying if I said I didn't find the idea tempting at first. Pushing myself back into shape and learning how to see again with only one working eye was painful, in all senses. *Would it be so bad to have a quiet day job?* I wondered. Becoming an agent was a chance to stay connected to the hockey world and put all of my knowledge of the game and the industry to use.

But deep down, I knew that wouldn't be enough for me. And each week, I was feeling better about myself. My depth perception was never going to be what it once was, but my hands were starting to get a feel for the puck again, and I was starting to turn and pivot a little faster, a little sharper on the ice. I knew that if I didn't give myself a serious shot at making a comeback, I'd always wonder about what could have been.

So I started testing out the idea with a few people I trusted. Brian Boucher was still playing in the NHL, and given that we went back a long way, I trusted his opinion. But his reaction wasn't quite what I was looking for.

"What if you hurt your good eye!" he said as soon as I told him.

"What if I do?" I said.

"That's a huge risk to take," Brian said.

"I know it is. But I have to try. If I don't, I'll always regret not pushing myself far enough."

Brian wasn't the only one who felt that way. But I told Tom and my family about my potential comeback, and the reactions were all roughly the same. They were all worried about the chance of me hurting my left eye.

Of course, I thought about that, too. I knew better than anyone that freak accidents like that could happen. But they could happen on or off the ice. I knew the risks involved in coming back, and they were risks I was willing to take.

Thinking that I could stage a comeback and actually making it happen were two very different things, though. My contract with the Leafs had expired. They paid me the whole time that I was hurt until the end of my contract, and my ties with the team ended in April 2001, when I received my final paycheck from them. I am certain that the Maple Leafs never thought a return to hockey was possible for me, and I wasn't saying much. I still didn't want to talk too much about my plan or even call it a comeback. If word got through to the Toronto press, they'd be all over the story, and I wasn't ready to be under that kind of spotlight. I still had to protect myself.

My break came when USA Hockey held a training camp to start building their team for the 2002 Winter Olympics. Herb Brooks was the coach of the team, and he and Tom went back a long time, to when Herb coached Tom on the Rangers. Tom asked Herb if I could come out and skate with the team. He made it clear that I knew I had no hope of making the USA Olympic team. My only goal was to prove to everyone that I could still play.

Herb said yes, and away I went to join the training camp in Colorado Springs, Colorado. What I didn't know at the time was that, at the same time, Tom had quietly reached out to a few teams to let them know that I was skating again. We figured that a new start in a new city would make things easier until I got back to where I used to be. So Tom contacted a few teams and told them to come out, watch me practice, and see how I was progressing.

The first day of the camp, I got to the dressing room before most of the guys arrived. It had been a year and a half since my injury. Eighteen months since I'd walked into a professional dressing room. So much had changed, and still, the moment I walked through the doors and breathed in the familiar sights and smells, I felt at ease.

Not long after I arrived, while I was stretching and getting ready, Brian Leetch walked into the room. The look on his face when he saw me was priceless—his jaw almost hit the floor.

"Hey, Leetchie," I said with a smile.

"B, what are you doing here?" he asked, giving me an energetic handshake.

"I've been working out and skating, so Tom asked Herb if I could come join the skate to see how I'm measuring up."

"That's great, man," Brian said. "How are you feeling?"

"Pretty good, all in all. The eye is as good as it is going to get, but my skating feels good."

Word got around quick that I was back, and as the other players came into the dressing room, they all came over to greet me and ask how I was doing. There were a lot of familiar faces, guys whom I had played with four years earlier in Nagano—Chris Chelios, Keith Tkachuk, Mike Modano, Brett Hull. Nobody had any advance warning that I'd be training with them. Leetch and the other guys at camp had read and heard all the stories that I was done, and they all assumed that was it.

I was a bit nervous when I hit the ice. For months I'd been skating by myself in familiar rinks. Now I was stepping back onto the ice with some of the best players in the world. I took a deep breath as I skated my first lap. *You can do this*, I thought.

That first practice, I felt like I couldn't miss with my passes. Of course, I was skating with the highest caliber of players out there—they could make any pass look good. A pass that would look awful to most players looks great when you are skating with players with that kind of talent. My vision was still a concern, and my timing was still off. But when it came to speed and strength, I was at the level of everyone else, and that felt amazing. I knew I had a long way to go, but I had made a big step in my comeback.

I was relieved to see that the progress I'd been making wasn't all in my head. I had lost some quickness, but my top speed was there. And I was convinced that my added size and strength would help to protect me if I got hit on my blind side.

Toward the end of camp, I stepped onto the ice for practice, and I noticed Leetch skating and stickhandling the puck with one eye closed.

"Leetchie, what are you doing?" I asked.

He shook his head. "B, I don't know how you are doing it with one eye, but you are doing it."

We both had a good laugh. Still, hearing from Leetch that I was able to keep up steeled my resolve. At the start of the camp, I'd wondered if playing in the NHL with one eye was even feasible. But by the end of the week, I knew I could do it. It was time to get back to the Show.

9

BROADWAY BRYAN

TOM'S DECISION TO INVITE A FEW GENERAL MANAGERS TO THE OLYMPIC CAMP ended up being incredibly savvy. Don Maloney, the assistant GM from the Rangers, was one of the few who showed up. He watched me practice and scrimmage, and a few days after camp, he called Tom.

"Bryan can still play," Don said. "I think we might have a spot for him."

I'm sure Tom was as surprised as everyone else. Tom and I figured the Olympic camp would just be a first step and a way of cracking open the door that might lead back to the NHL. We were prepared for it to take months, or even another season, before a team took a chance and signed me.

I must have made a better impression than I thought, because a few weeks later, Glen Sather, the GM of the Rangers, called. He was going to give me a shot.

When Tom gave me the news, I was so fired up.

"Let's do it!" I said. "Where do I sign?"

"Not so fast, Bryan," Tom said. "We have a few important things we need to discuss."

Tom sat me down for a serious talk. He explained that, if I wanted to make a serious comeback, it meant I would have to pay back all of the money from my insurance payments: $6.3 million.

"That's going to take a long time," Tom said. "You're not the same player you were before, so the offers aren't going to be the same."

The insurance companies would give me a three-year window to pay back all of the $6 million. Tom was both honest and supportive.

"Just be patient and keep at it," he said with a smile. "We'll get you there."

I appreciated Tom's honesty about the offers he expected. But this wasn't about the money for me—I would have paid back all of the insurance money and then some if it meant I got to play in the NHL again.

Because I was disabled permanently with my eye injury, I should have been able to keep the $6 million portion of the insurance settlement. As a result of my eye injury, I was disabled for life, whether or not I ever went back to the NHL.

My personal insurance policy was written by Lloyd's of London, and they slipped a clause into the medical release that I had signed. My attorney didn't read over the document as carefully as he should have, and he missed that clause.

Years after my career ended, my lawyer contacted the insurance company and said we felt that we had the case to get the money that was owed to me as a result of the injury. The insurance company responded by suing me in the state of New York.

The first judge threw the case out because I had signed the release and, even though I had legal representation, he felt I never should have signed the release. The case went to an appeals court, where one of the judges voted in my favor, while the other two ruled against me. They said that I should have known better.

The first year I was back in the NHL with the Rangers, my salary was going to be $2 million. Ironically, my first installment to the insurance company was also $2 million.

The plan was clear. With every due date, I would take whatever money I'd earned from my paychecks and send it to the insurance company. I hadn't even played a regular season game for the Rangers yet, and I had to cut a check for $2 million to start repaying the insurance policy. From a financial standpoint, it was a terrible decision to come back and play in the NHL. But I was back, and that was what mattered to me.

• • •

Once Tom was sure I was committed to that path, he put things in motion. I waited back in Rhode Island while he negotiated, and in September 2001, the Rangers presented me with a standard NHL contract for $2 million.

Even though I was technically back in the NHL, I was far from being the same player I was before my injury. If I was being honest, I was barely 50 percent of the player that I was before. I would still need a lot of ice time and repetition to get my skills and timing back to the level they needed to be at.

I was lucky that the organization I was stepping into was ready to support me however I needed. I showed up in town with just my hockey gear and a couple of suitcases, and I checked into a hotel. I would eventually rent an apartment in the city, but in the meantime, my focus was on one thing and one thing only: hockey.

The Rangers were led by Mark Messier, and from the moment I joined the team, he made sure I knew I was part of the Rangers family. Mark had an aura about him—once you were a part of the team, you were immediately accepted, no questions asked.

Early into training camp that September, Mark and Brian Leetch sat down with me for an honest conversation. We sat around late into the night, talking about my injury and my comeback. I was very honest about what I was going through and the frustrations that I had been experiencing.

Throughout it all, Mark spoke like we'd been teammates for years. He wanted to know how I was feeling, what parts of my game I was feeling good about, and where the team might need to support me.

The final thing that Mark said to me, though, really stuck with me. "Just go play," he said. "There's going to be some frustration along the way. That's natural. You just go play and the rest will follow."

Go play, I kept repeating to myself afterward. *Words to live by in hockey and in life.*

Mark and Brian were right. Every practice and every game that followed, I went out and tried to focus only on improving some small part of my game. One day, I concentrated on making sure I was picking up the puck smoothly along the boards. Another, my goal was to make sure every pass hit the tape of the next guy's stick. The next practice, I was trying to dial in my slap shot and put the puck in the same spot of the net on each and every shot.

There were frustrations, just like they said there would be. My depth perception was always going to be an issue. When the puck was on the ice, as it usually was, I didn't have too many issues. There were enough other reference points—the boards, other players, the reach of my stick—for me to be able to track it properly. But when the puck was in the air or if someone did a flip pass, I was in trouble. I had to concentrate really hard to find the puck when it was up in the air. Too many times, I would lose it in the glass and the lights. *So much for all of those games of catch with Greg and Bruce*, I thought every time it happened.

The most frustrating thing about coming back, though, was wearing a visor. I hated wearing a visor. When I first made the NHL, ditching my visor had been the first equipment change I'd made. Now, though, I simply had no choice. I had to wear a visor to protect my one good eye.

It wasn't just wearing the visor that bugged me, though. It was how close I had to keep it to my face. My first practice, I showed the trainers how tight I needed the visor. They looked at me like I was crazy—no one else kept it that close to their face—but they helped me out.

Unlike other players, my visor was almost touching my nose and cheekbone in order to create this tight seal around my face. Because it was so close, it would fog up on me after every shift. The last thing I needed was something else obscuring my vision on the ice, so I would sit on the bench after each shift, my face hot and claustrophobic, trying desperately to wipe off the fog.

For the first few games, I was constantly grumbling between shifts about the visor cutting into my nose or fogging up. The other guys were patient with me, but eventually, they had enough. After one game, Brian came up to me and said, "B, enough about the visor. You're back in the NHL. Think about everything you've put yourself through to get back to this point. Stop complaining and deal with it."

That set me straight, and I never complained about the visor after that. I tried not to complain about anything from them on, even the lessons that really hurt.

One night, we were in Minnesota and ESPN was broadcasting the game. I got hit along the boards near the benches, and I was knocked off-balance. The camera guy by the bench couldn't get out of the way in time, and as I fell to the ice, my head smoked the camera between the benches.

The impact split my helmet and cut the top of my skull. I stood up, and I was seeing stars. I slowly made my way to our bench, blood trickling down my face. The trainers took me into the back room, but seven stitches later, I was back on the bench, ready to get back into the game.

For the rest of the night, my good eye was seeing these fuzzy lines, but I wrote it off to just another side issue from my eye injury. I later learned that I suffered a concussion, and that I shouldn't have been playing the rest of that night, but at the time, I just told myself, "It could be worse," and I carried on.

Throughout the season, moments like that taught me that I wasn't going to have to overhaul just the small parts of my game—I'd have to rethink the entire way I played the game. No longer could I jump into the play as an offensive defenseman. Every time I tried that in preseason, I was half a step behind, or I hesitated just a little bit—enough time for the opposing team to close in on me or for me to stickhandle my way into trouble.

The first year back with the Rangers, I felt fear on the ice for the first time ever. Up until then, I had never been nervous about getting hurt while I was playing hockey. But now I was getting anxious when a stick accidentally flew high or a puck deflected off a stick. What if one of them struck my good eye?

I just didn't have the confidence to grab the puck and skate into the offensive zone the way I had before. I started to become more of a stay-at-home defenseman. If I couldn't move the puck myself, I'd make sure I read the play and made the right pass at the right time. My sight on the ice had gotten worse, but in a way, I was seeing the game clearer than ever before.

Still, any player who suffers an injury—any injury—finds their first year back a major struggle. One night, in January 2002, I was feeling good about myself. We were playing the Devils in New Jersey, and I thought the time was right to try something new.

Big mistake.

We were on the power play, and I had the puck. I didn't see a clear pass to the wings or shot on net. John Madden, a Rangers forward, was pressuring me, and I tried to toe-drag around him.

A few years before, I would have been able to do it. But I misjudged the distance that John had to close between us. He picked my pocket and set up Jay Pandolfo for a shorthanded goal.

I slammed my stick on the ice after the puck went in. We ended up losing the game 6–4, and I felt entirely responsible for the loss.

After the game, Glen Sather came storming up to me.

"If you ever do something like that again, you're going to be fucking sitting," he said.

Then he turned around and marched right back out of the room.

I felt my face going red. I was pissed off at myself for making such a stupid play, and I knew I had cost us the game. I deserved to be yelled at. *Maybe this comeback wasn't such a great idea*, I thought.

Then I felt a tap on my knee. I looked up and saw Leetch leaning over.

"Don't worry about it, B," he said. "We win and lose as a team. Back to work tomorrow."

I couldn't have made it through that year without the support of my teammates, friends, and family. I still called my parents and siblings almost every day. Hearing their voices always helped to calm me down.

Still, even with their support, the year was mentally draining. Each day, when I woke up and opened my eyes, I was immediately reminded of what I was battling against. I reminded myself to savor the little things. Every small victory—a game without a giveaway, a thread-the-needle pass—took on new significance.

Finally, in February 2002, I scored my first goal since I came back. We were playing Philadelphia, and I came into the Flyers' zone on a one-on-two. I broke through the defense, and as I closed in on their goalie, Roman Cechmanek, he came out to poke-check me. I tried to deke around him, but I lost the handle on the puck. Luckily, the puck rolled through Cechmanek's five-hole as he skated out.

The moment I saw the puck cross the line, I felt a surge of confidence flow through me. I remembered what a rush it was to see your teammates skate toward you, their arms in the air in celebration and the crowd cheering around you. For the first time in a while, I completely forgot about my injury.

Living in Manhattan was also a welcome change from the quiet year I'd spent in Rhode Island. There was a real cast of characters on the team that year—Eric Lindros, Pavel Bure, Theo Fleury. Messier was a god in New York City. Whenever we went out for dinner, he would get escorted past whatever line there was. People would clear out of the way when he walked down the street—he was the alpha, and New Yorkers couldn't get enough of him.

Despite our star power that year, we didn't have a great season on the ice. Our record wasn't as good as we wanted, and we missed the playoffs.

As the season was winding down, I thought back on how the last few months had gone. I knew that I was still struggling to process the game at a high speed. Before my eye injury, it seemed as though I could read and find the play in a split second. It was almost second nature—I would get the puck and know instinctively what to do with it or where to pass it. Now, though, it was still taking me a quarter to a half a second to make a play. Not a long time objectively, but an eternity in an NHL game.

Still, I was proud that I played all eighty-two games that first year back. I was the sixth defenseman on the team, but I didn't mind. I gave credit to Glen Sather and Ron Low for sticking with me for the entire season.

I didn't think my place on the ice was hurting the Rangers, but at the same time, I recognized that I wasn't helping them that much offensively. I scored only one more goal that season, and although I managed to rack up twenty-three points, that was a far cry from the kinds of numbers that I was putting up before my injury.

I was determined to keep improving my game, and I felt like getting a full season under my belt was a step in the right direction. I wasn't ready for the season to be over. I'd played eighty-two games, and I wanted more. "Go play," Messier said. I was ready to do exactly that, wherever it took me.

10

EARNING A LIVING

AFTER ONE SEASON WITH THE RANGERS, TOM APPROACHED GLEN SATHER, the team's GM, about extending my contract. They had a good talk, but ultimately, the Rangers weren't interested in re-signing me.

Tom went right back to work, though, and I headed back to Rhode Island to work on my strength. Later that summer of 2002, the hard work of both of us was rewarded when the Boston Bruins signed me to a one-year, free-agent contract.

When I arrived at training camp that fall, one of the first things the Bruins' training staff and fitness coaches did was put us through the bench press test to see how strong we were.

The king of the Bruins' weight room that year was Martin Lapointe, with Michael Grosek close behind. Marty wasn't tall, but as soon as I saw his big arms and barrel-shaped chest, I knew he was incredibly strong.

John Whiteside, the Bruins' strength coach, set up the bench press with a weight that we said we could handle.

Of course, when it was Marty's turn, he loaded the bar up to 225 pounds and went to work. He did more than thirty reps at that weight and barely broke a sweat doing it.

After watching Marty do his thing, I made sure I did one less rep than he did. I was eager to prove to everyone that I was in good shape. But I was also new to the Bruins, and I didn't want to ruffle any feathers.

When I was with the Rangers, I was 50 percent of what I used to be before I hurt my eye. At the start of the season in Boston, I was feeling closer to 70 percent of my full capacity. Being the best you can be at hockey is the same as any other pursuit—it takes a lot of practice and a lot of repetition. I had a year since my return under my belt, but I was still playing catch-up.

My stall that year was next to Brian Rolston's. One day, we were lacing up our skates, when Rolston looked over and said, "B, when did you get that tattoo?"

He nodded at the tattoo on my right shoulder. It was a bad image of a gargoyle that is sitting on the sun, which has a pair of eyes. The gargoyle was biting the sun's right eye.

"I got it when I was seventeen," I said.

Rolston stared at the tattoo, then looked up at my face. "That. Is. Weird," he said.

I stood up and looked in the mirror to get a good look at what Brian was talking about. Then I realized: the gargoyle was biting the sun's right eye. The same one that I'd injured. It was eerie.

By this time in my career, I was getting more comfortable with life in the NHL. I had a feel for the rhythm of the game and I understood what I needed to endure the day-to-day grind: the nutrition, the conditioning, the coaching. And, of course, the fun.

We made sure to tap into that fun atmosphere throughout the rest of the season. During the week, we went to work and did everything we could to win, night in and night out. But most Sundays, when we didn't have games, I'd head to a bar with some of the guys from the team. We'd hang out in a private room in the upper level, watch football, and bet on the games. But the best part was at the end of the day, when we'd put on the newest episode of *The Sopranos*. I loved the show, and I was a huge fan of the Tony Soprano character. Providence, Rhode Island, had a big Italian community when I was growing up, and there were even a few mob bosses who had come out of there. My friends and had all heard about a few Tony Soprano types when we were growing up.

I enjoyed those Sundays in Boston, but unlike a lot of guys in the league, I never minded away games. Every team is an odd mash-up of twenty or so adults, each of whom has a different habit and routine for how they live their life and get ready for work. My favorite thing to do was go out for dinner the night before a game. Other guys wanted to just chill out with a bunch of movies in their hotel room.

Either way, road trips were a chance for each of us to get to know the quirks of the rest of the guys on the team. When we were on the road, there were no distractions and we were forced to spend more time together. It was the perfect way to bond with new teammates.

That sort of bonding was helpful in the long term, too. When you got down to it, the NHL was a business, which meant that, no matter how much you cared about the guys beside you in a season, there was no guarantee you wouldn't be traded or re-signed elsewhere. Anything could change on a moment's notice.

When I was playing in the NHL, there were no friends on the ice. When it came time to play, even if you'd known a guy your entire life, you would still hit him, run him into the boards, maybe even fight him. After the game, you could have a beer and move on. But on the ice, every time we played the Flyers, there was never a moment when I wasn't trying as hard as I could to score on Brian. The fact that we'd been friends since childhood didn't matter—I would do anything I could to score, and he'd do everything he could to stop me.

Hanging out with teammates between games, getting to know them and their families, and bonding with each other wasn't just a way of getting closer as a team and winning together. It was also our safety net. It ensured that, if you were traded or had to move somewhere, you had a relationship with the guys from your previous team. The next time you saw each other, even if it was from opposite sides of the face-off circle, you knew the people wearing the other team's jersey.

Having already played for so many teams, I had come to appreciate that system. But I didn't know just how soon I'd rely on it again.

At the end of the season, a bunch of us took a trip to Las Vegas. When the Hard Rock Casino found out we were coming down, they sent a private jet to pick us up and fly us to Vegas.

We ended up spending a lot of time in Vegas with a big Boston Bruins fan we met. He was a Greek guy who was high up in the finance industry, and he was the first legitimate high roller that I had ever met.

The first time I saw the guy head to the tables, I watched him drop $30,000 on a single hand of baccarat, the same card game that James

Bond often plays in the movies. My jaw hit the floor. *That's over half a year's pay for my dad*, I thought. I always gave myself a budget for what I was willing to spend on a night at the casino, and it was well south of what our host was betting on each hand. I was still paying back my insurance settlement, and I couldn't afford to go overboard.

I went back to Las Vegas later that summer for Jerry Bruckheimer's "The Bad Boys of Hockey." It was a regular event where Jerry brought together actors, like Cuba Gooding, Jr., and Tim Robbins, and players for a friendly series of games. It was a refreshing escape, and a nice way to round out the summer. Chris Chelios and Sergei Fedorov were there as well. That was a great time and I ended up taking part in the event for a number of years.

That same summer in 2003, I invited Brian Boucher to join me in a golf tournament. It was a pro-am event where NHL players were teamed up with senior golfers from the Champions Tour, and all of the proceeds went to the Cam Neely Foundation.

Brian laughed when I told him about the event. Brian was a good golfer with a smooth swing, but I didn't start playing regularly until I was around nineteen. Brian was always making fun of me, but I was determined to prove that I could hold my own on the course.

I was so nervous as I teed up on the first hole—far more so than I had ever been dressing for a hockey game.

There were galleries all around the tee box that were full of fans, and as I set up my tee, the event organizers announced my name, just like a real tour event. I felt myself begin to sweat. When I played hockey, I relished the boos from the other team's fans and I got pumped up by the energy of the crowd—it always made me focus more and perform better. That sure didn't carry through to my golf game, though. I hooked a four-iron off the tee out of bounds and had to tee up another ball and try again.

After that, I relaxed. Apart from that disaster on the opening hole, it was probably one of the better rounds of golf I ever had. Brian was in the group behind me, so I knew I had to keep it up or he'd never let me hear the end of it.

Finally, we made it to the eighteenth hole. I had an easy shot to the green, and my caddy handed me my wedge.

"Last shot of the day, Bryan," he said. "Let's make it a good one."

"Absolutely," I said.

I lined up my shot, swung through, and absolutely skulled the ball.

The crowd made let out a disappointed, "Ohhh," as the ball flew along the ground. But it quickly turned into an, "Oh, no!" The fans positioned around the green scattered as the ball came screaming at them. It bounced all over the aluminum seats and ended up at the back of the grandstand, where it landed on the TV announcers' table next to one of their monitors.

Because my ball was on the TV table, I was able to get a free drop, so I managed to salvage the hole and my round. But it was a humbling experience. When Brian found out what had happened, we had a good laugh about it.

"It's a good thing you made it back to hockey," he said, slapping me on the back. "I'm not sure a career as a pro golfer is in the cards for you."

•   •   •

I had earned $850,000 the last season in Boston—the same amount as I had as a rookie—and I ended up with ten goals and thirty-eight points in eighty games played.

I'd only signed a one-year contract, so I was due for a contract negotiation with the team. Things didn't go as smoothly as I would have liked. It wasn't personal—strictly business. I got the sense that Boston didn't want to lose me, but they did want me to sign at a discounted price. I'd become accustomed to this sort of thing. It was part of playing in the NHL. Teams wanted to sign players for as little as possible, while players, knowing their careers weren't long, tried to earn as much as they could while they played.

Tom and I ended up going to arbitration with the Bruins to settle the dispute. The arbitrator awarded us $2.5 million—that was going to be my price tag for the next year. I felt it was fair, given what I could provide to the team, but general manager Mike O'Connell and the Bruins walked away from the deal.

"It's a gamble," Tom said to me. "They're hoping you'll cave and accept a lower offer."

According to the rules of the CBA at the time, any other team that signed me had to pay me more than what I was awarded by the arbitrator. Tom figured the Bruins were betting that no other team would be willing to pay me more than the $2.5 million we were given by the arbitrator. It wasn't callous; it was just business.

I was bummed out, waiting to find out what team, if any, would sign me. I had already missed so much time recovering from eye injury; I didn't want to miss any more waiting for a new contract.

One week into the 2003–04 season, I still didn't have a team.

"How long should we wait for?" I asked Tom.

"Give it another week or two," he said. "Teams are going to be shaking up their lineups, either because they have injuries or because they don't have the right mix of guys. When that happens, we'll get you a deal."

As always, Tom was right. It took a few more weeks, but on October 31, 2003, I signed with the Chicago Blackhawks for $2.51 million.

I was excited to finally have a team to play for, and I immediately headed to Chicago to report. On the flight there, Tom filled me in on the situation. It was shaping up to be a challenging year for the Blackhawks. They were a young team that had just missed the playoffs the year before. They'd only won three of their first eleven games, and I was one of the few veterans on the team, along with Ryan VandenBussche, Jason Strudwick, Eric Daze, and Jocelyn Thibault.

The coach for the Blackhawks that year was Brian Sutter. He had a reputation for being tough on the young players. Fortunately for me, I got along with Brian well—we seemed to be on the same wavelength.

As soon as I got to Chicago, Sutter was talking my ear off about the young players. If he saw me in the morning, he would call me in his office. I soon learned that, once that happened, I wasn't going anywhere. I'd be stuck there for thirty minutes as Brian sipped his morning coffee and talked about whatever was on his mind—the way the league was headed, how there was no "heart" in the NHL anymore. I liked Brian Sutter a lot, and I respected him, so I always listened and let him get what he had to say off his chest. I felt like his therapist. Most of the time, he was right on with what he was saying, and I could see how the style of play in the league was changing the way he called it. Still, the chats could sometimes drag on, so some mornings, I'd try to sneak past his office so that I could have a quiet coffee before practice.

After the year in Boston, I felt I needed some kind of change to shake up my routines a bit. I had worn number 34 all through my NHL career—it was the number I was given when I showed up to play for the Detroit Junior Red Wings, and I'd never had the urge to change it, not even after my injury.

When I joined the Blackhawks, I asked for number 3. In December of that year, though, Keith Magnuson was killed in a car accident. Magnuson had played for the Blackhawks all through the seventies, and he'd worn number 3 during his career.

Keith Magnuson was beloved in Chicago, and we were all devastated by the news of his death, so I didn't feel right wearing his number anymore. I called Chris Chelios to ask his advice. Chelios was the godfather of hockey in the United States, and when in doubt, you called Chelly. He agreed that changing my number was the right move to respect the Magnuson family, so I switched my jersey to number 4.

Not everything was tough in Chicago that year, though. One of the nicest things about that season was being paired with Jason Strudwick. Struddy and I had played together with the Islanders at the start of my career, and I knew he was a guy I could trust, on and off the ice.

The first time Strudwick and I played together on the Islanders, he'd just been called up from our AHL affiliate. After that game, he mentioned how he wanted to go into New York City. I tossed him the keys to my car—a Lexus SC400 Coupe—and told him to have fun.

That year in Chicago, Struddy repaid that favor many times over. I was a risk-taking, one-eyed defenseman, so mistakes happened.

Some of the younger guys that year joked with me, saying that

I was doing things on the ice with one eye that they couldn't do with two.

"What's your secret?" they'd ask.

"Vision," I said. They laughed their heads off, thinking I was joking. But I wasn't. The only way I was able to keep performing at the highest level possible was to keep my head on a swivel and continue to reteach myself how to see the game differently, as I'd started to do with the Rangers. Angles became more important, as did reading guys' body language. I needed to know a split second earlier whether my winger was going to cut to the outside or the inside if I was going to hit him with a pass. Reading the play properly could lead to a goal. If I couldn't preempt the play, though, I'd inevitably be dealing with the consequences back around our own net.

I wanted to avoid being back on my heels as much as possible. It was defensively where my eye injury affected my play the most. In the defensive zone, I always had to be on guard. The puck would be bouncing all over the place and players were flying around—it was a big challenge to track the play and keep everything in focus.

I didn't mind if another team's player was forechecking me, because I could feel where he was. I could hear what direction his skates were coming from or the tap of his stick, and I only had to focus on one direction.

It was when two players were on me that I struggled. Guys were respectful about it, though, especially the other veterans. They would still check me into the boards, but they almost always gave me a heads-up what was about to happen and what side they were on so that I wasn't injured.

Before I hurt my eye, I never heard one player ever say, "Look out,

I'm coming on your left." Guys would just run you and it was on you
to get out of the way. Since my return, though, most guys were good
about giving me a fighting chance, and I appreciated the respect.

We had an assistant coach that year by the name of Al MacAdam.
Al ran the defense for the Blackhawks, while Denis Savard coached
the forwards. I was feeling good that year and putting up points, so I
decided to try to expand my range of skills. In one of my morning talks
with Brian, I ran the idea by him.

"Brian," I said when I could get a word in, "I know I play a lot on
the power play, but I'd like to try killing penalties."

Brian raised an eyebrow. "Interesting idea," he said. "You sure? It's
a lot different than playing on the man advantage."

"I'm sure," I said. "I'd like a new challenge."

Brian grinned. "Let me talk to Al."

A few weeks later, we were in St. Louis, and we had to kill off a
five-on-three.

"B, get out there," Al said, tapping me on the back. I didn't hesitate
and leaped over the boards for the penalty kill.

It seemed to be going well—or, at least, the puck wasn't going in
our net—when one of the St. Louis forwards took a one-timer from the
point. I was standing in the slot, and I saw the puck rising. Everything
seemed to be in slow motion, and I had no time to react. *It's headed
right for my eye*, was all I could think.

It was close. The puck hit the bottom of my visor and deflected
into my jaw. I skated back to the bench and while I wasn't in agony, it
didn't feel great. As I sat down on the bench and tried to shake off the
pain, Al walked up to me and said, "How do you like killing penalties
now, Berard?"

I started laughing after he said that, and that just made my jaw hurt more. After the game, I finally went for X-rays, and I discovered I had a hairline fracture in my jaw. *Maybe no more penalty kills for a little while*, I thought.

We didn't make the playoffs that year, but when the season ended, I was still happier than I had been in a long time. Brian Sutter played me a lot, and he encouraged me to shoot the puck. He encouraged me to shoot to discourage opposing players from trying to block shots. His theory was that if people feared my shot and would hesitate to block it, more pucks would get through to the net on the power play. Between that and playing with really talented guys like Steve Sullivan, Stephane Robidas, and Alexei Zhamnov on the power play, and I was almost a point-per-game player that year. Robidas, in particular, was a big reason why I was able to put up so many points in Chicago that year. He was a right-hand shot, and I shot left, so we were able to zip the puck around to each other on the power play and open up lots of great shots for each other.

I knew a lot of other guys on the team would be coming back the next year, and the more I talked about it with Tom, the more we felt that Chicago would be a great fit for me. I loved the city, too, and I was looking forward to not having to move again.

Late in the season, I was told that the Blackhawks had nominated me for the Bill Masterton Memorial Trophy. It is given out each year to the player who best demonstrates perseverance, sportsmanship, and dedication to hockey. The season before, Steve Yzerman had won it, and some of the names from previous years—Ken Daneyko, Gary Roberts, Pat Lafontaine—were among the best of the best. I was humbled just to be considered among them.

That turned to outright disbelief at the end of the season, when I learned that I was a finalist for the award that year.

As I sat in the audience the night of the awards, I thought back to the last time I'd been at the event, just after my rookie year. Then, as now, I was proud to be recognized by my colleagues, whom I respected so much. But this time around, the night felt different. I had a new perspective. The awards were appreciated and an accomplishment to be proud of. But they weren't what was most important in life. Family, friends, giving back to the people around you — those were what mattered most. I wanted to win the Stanley Cup with every bone in my body, and I would have given everything to get there. But as I looked around the room and saw the elite talent around me, I felt proud at what I had accomplished and what I had gone through to be there that night.

The one major difference with the Bill Masterton is that, unlike, say, the Calder, they tell the winner in advance of the ceremony. My first reaction was excitement at the honor, but it was quickly replaced with a feeling of dread — I would have to give a speech again.

Luckily, I had some advance notice this time, which gave me an opportunity to prepare my acceptance speech. My family still teased me about how bad my speech was when I won the Calder, and I didn't want to repeat the same mistake.

When it came time to give the speech, I kept it short and sweet to reduce the chances of screwing it up. I spoke about the long road I'd faced getting back to hockey, and I thanked everyone who had helped me along the way — the doctors, fans, team members, and, most important, my family. When I was healing, my family and I had been overwhelmed by letters, get-well cards, and homemade posters from fans wishing me a speedy recovery. Every single one of them had touched us and helped me along my recovery, and my mom had helped me respond to as many as we could. I had been humbled that people I'd never met cared that much, and I tried to convey what I felt—that every single person who'd taken the time like that shared in the award with me.

There was no way I could express the depth of my gratitude to everyone. The rest of the night, every time I looked at the trophy in my hands, the room around me fell away, replaced with my parents' home, where I'd grown up as a kid and where I had put myself back together as an adult. I was humbled to even be holding the award, and I made a silent promise to myself that I'd try to live up to what it represented, every single day.

•   •   •

Before the season ended, Tom had made an agreement with Bob Pulford, the Blackhawks GM, for me to sign a new contract and stay in Chicago for three more years. But I couldn't sign it. It wasn't because I didn't want to—quite the opposite. The problem was the NHL lockout. When the lockout began, no deals of any kind could be signed. Everything went on indefinite hold.

Still, I focused on the positives. I was happy about the deal we had in principle, and I liked the city of Chicago. I knew the organization was in the process of turning the Blackhawks into a winner again. All I had to do was wait for the lockout to end and I could sign the deal.

With no end to the lockout in sight, I decided to move to Manhattan Beach, California. Because of the lockout, I wasn't making any money. I was living off of my savings and investments. Considering the cost of living in California, it probably would have been smarter for me to stay in Rhode Island and save some money. But I had just broken up with my girlfriend in Rhode Island, and I needed a change of scenery.

I moved in with Steve Shields, one of my former teammates in Boston, and we started training with T. R. Goodman at Gold's Gym in Venice Beach. Chris Chelios, Rob Blake, Chris Simon, and a bunch of other guys also worked out with Goodman. That year, Mike Comrie and Danny Cleary were my training partners, and the three of us were always at the gym.

Goodman was a good trainer, but he was a big believer in using heavy weights to build up your legs. At first, I loved the new approach, but after a while, I could feel the strain starting to eat away at my lower back. I tried to change things up by playing basketball and a little beach volleyball, but I couldn't seem to shake the stiffness. I told myself it was temporary—I'd be back on the ice soon.

Unfortunately, the lockout ended up wiping out the entire 2004–05 season. It was disappointing for everyone in the league. It was the first time since 1919 that the Stanley Cup hadn't been awarded, and the first time a major professional sports league in North America had canceled a complete season because of a labor dispute.

Just before the lockout was officially ended in July 2005, Tom and I got some news that made things even more difficult. The Blackhawks had fired Pulford and hired Dale Tallon to be their new GM in his place.

When the lockout was officially ended, Tom broke the news to me: Dale Tallon had pulled the contract offer. To this day, I still don't know why that happened.

I didn't have time to feel bad for myself, though. I needed to find a place to play.

A few weeks later, I got a call from Doug MacLean, the GM for the Columbus Blue Jackets, offering me a two-year deal close to the one I was going to sign in Chicago. I was thrilled to not only be playing again that season, but to have the promise of another year with the same team after that.

I was also excited at the prospect of another year of making a living in hockey. When I signed with the Columbus Blue Jackets, I had just paid off the insurance company from my eye injury settlement. The 2005–06 season with Columbus, then, would mark the first time since my return that I was able to make a living for myself again, rather than for the insurance company.

I moved to downtown Columbus that summer and started to get acquainted with my new hometown. The first few weeks I spent exploring the city, I realized that this was going to be a lot different than living in Chicago or Boston. Many of the married players on the team had settled down outside the city center in Dublin, Ohio. Ohio State was in Columbus, and there were a lot of college bars around the city, so for the older players, living outside the city was a chance for a little more peace and quiet.

I was thirty years old, and I knew I couldn't be hanging out at those college bars with the young guys on the team. But there wasn't much going on for a single guy living downtown beyond that scene. I spent most of my time watching TV, going out to dinner, and just hanging out. There was only so much I could do to fill my time, though, so more often than not, I went back to the gym or the rink to keep training. If I wasn't at the gym, I was the tattoo shop, working on my full-length sleeves.

At this point in my career, I took off-season training more seriously than I ever had. I could still feel my body working against me at times, and any time I stepped away from my conditioning for too long, I could feel my strength start to slide back to where it was right after my injury. My eye injury might have healed years before, but the effect it had on my body was still ongoing.

In September 2005, I attended the Team USA evaluation camp in Colorado Springs, Colorado. I'd been named to the preliminary roster for the U.S. Olympic Team that was gearing up for the Turin Games the next year. I didn't see any way that Team USA was going to take me to the Winter Olympics—I was honored they'd even invited me to the preliminary evaluation.

As part of the team's Olympic preparations, there was going to be a series of random, no-advance-notice tests carried out by the United States Anti-Doping Agency (USADA) and the World Anti-Doping Agency (WADA) in the weeks and months that followed. The organizations conducted tests for banned substances—specifically, they were looking for performance-enhancing drugs.

A few months earlier, in July 2005, the NHL had announced that it was going to start testing its players for performance-enhancing drugs for the first time. When I'd heard that, I had immediately gone to my NHLPA rep and told them and the organization's doctors about what I was taking, when I took it, and why.

"Are you still taking steroids?" the rep asked.

"No," I said truthfully. "I stopped a few months ago."

"Then you should be fine. Because you stopped so long ago, everything should be out of your system by the time the testing starts."

I was relieved. I'd stopped taking the steroids months ago and didn't intend to resume taking them. My body was back in shape and was staying healthy, and I didn't want to mess with that.

When it came time for my USADA-run test in November 2005, then, I figured the drugs were out of my system and that there wouldn't be any issues. But when my test results came back, the result was a positive match: the test had found performance-enhancing drugs in my system.

When I got the test results, Tom and I reached out to WADA. We told them that I wasn't making the Olympic team—the roster had almost been finalized, and I knew I wasn't at the level I needed to be to make it. We asked if I could use the incident as a teaching moment, doing public service announcements for kids about the perils of using performance-enhancing drugs. I didn't want the news to come out in the public. I had called my parents and broken the news to them, but I was worried about the impact the news might have on fans—I didn't want them to think poorly of the NHL or the U.S. Olympic program.

But WADA was firm: they wanted to publicize the results, especially as they related to a pro athlete. Despite their earlier announcement, the NHL didn't yet have a rule making steroids illegal in the league. I was suspended from participating in the World Hockey Championships or any other international competitions for two years. The next thing I knew, I was getting calls from the media asking about it and the Associated Press was reporting about it.

I decided to be perfectly honest. Jason Giambi of the New York Yankees had gone through a similar experience recently, and I'd been impressed by his honesty afterward, so I decided to follow in his footsteps. I didn't want the story to get any bigger than it already was, so I went to the media and admitted everything. I explained that I had been coming back from a horrific injury that had taken a huge and ongoing toll on my body. I told anyone who asked the truth: I had consulted with a doctor, and following that advice, I had decided to take steroids all on my own. It had been a way through the trauma from my eye injury and to get my body back to a place where I had enough strength to protect myself from any potential injury.

I took full responsibility for my actions, and I knew I'd made a mistake in taking the steroids in the first place. And I swore that I would never touch them again.

A few weeks after I tested positive with the USADA, I got in touch with the NHLPA. I asked to be tested again to make sure that the drugs were out of my system. The results that time were negative: the test didn't find any performance-enhancing substances.

I'd learned a hard lesson. If I was going to keep playing the game I loved, there was no room for steroids or other enhancements. I had paid the price. At least, I thought I had. But there was more to come.

•　　•　　•

During my time in Columbus, my back began to hurt. It started as a dull ache a few times a week. I would treat it whenever it arose and deal with it through stretching or physio in order to play. But dealing with that didn't remove the pain entirely—it just held it at bay for a little while. With each passing day, the issue got worse. By December 2005, I was in agony every day.

Most days, my back hurt so badly that I could barely bend over to put on socks and underwear. It got to the point that I wouldn't wear underwear or socks to the rink. The guys on the team all teased me because I'd show up to the rink wearing jeans and a pair of Uggs—the easiest shoes I could find for slipping on without bending over. The guys on the team had a field day with my style choices.

I got close to having to ask the trainers to tie my skates for me. When that thought crossed my mind, I decided it was time to figure out the cause of the problem once and for all.

The team doctors did an MRI, and it showed that I had a bulging disc in my lower back.

I took a few games off at the end of December to try to work the disc back into place. I felt a little better. *Maybe I just needed a bit of rest*, I thought. I made it back in the lineup, and I felt everything was going to be fine.

At the end of January, we were playing the Minnesota Wild. We were on a five-on-three power play, and I was set up on the point in my usual spot. My winger fed me the puck, and I wound up for a one-timer. I scored the goal, but my celebration was short-lived. As I followed through on the shot, leaning all my weight into it, I felt something pop in my back.

I immediately went back to the bench. I tried to stretch a little bit and let my body relax. A minute or two later, I was back on the ice and the puck came to me at center ice. I leaned over to play the puck, and just that small movement felt like somebody had shot me in the back with a shotgun.

I fell to my knees, and I couldn't get back up. They called the play dead, and one of the linesmen had to get behind me and push me over to our bench. From there, I crawled back to the locker room on all fours.

The doctors examined me that night and decided to send me for an MRI the next day. After the test, the doctors broke the news: I had herniated my L3–L4 discs in my lower back.

"What can I do to avoid back surgery?" I asked the doctors. I knew that the surgery would mean my season was over, and I wasn't ready for that to happen.

The doctors exchanged a quick look. "I'm sorry, Bryan," one of them said. "There's no other option."

I tried getting a second opinion from a back specialist in Los Angeles, Dr. Watkins. But he had the same opinion: if I was going to repair the damage, it was surgery or nothing.

I had no choice but to accept my fate. I had the surgery in January, and with that, I was out for the rest of the season.

After the surgery, I did feel better. Movements that had previously been unbearably painful, I could now do without discomfort. Eventually I was recovered enough to start training again. Surgery on my eye hadn't stopped me from getting back into the NHL; this certainly wasn't going to, either.

My mom always told my siblings and me, "Things could be worse." I tried to keep that in mind as I was recovering and rehabilitating, but every so often, I needed a reminder.

There was a restaurant I often went to in Columbus, and one of the waitresses there had some amazing tattoos. I asked her where she got them done, and it turned out her boyfriend was a tattoo artist by the name of Naryan.

I went to see Naryan, and we began working on a sleeve of tattoos for me. There were a number of images and word in the artwork, but one of the most important to me was a James Dean quote that was going to sit on my left arm: "Dream as if you'll live forever. Live as if you'll die today." The words struck a chord with me, and every time I looked down at them, I was inspired to keep moving forward.

• • •

I trained extra hard throughout that summer, doing everything I could to get ready for the next season. By the time training camp rolled around in September 2006, I felt I was ready to go for my second season in Columbus.

The second I started up again at camp, though, all my symptoms returned. I was in enough pain that I was back on my knees, barely able to skate properly each day.

I went back and underwent more testing with Dr. Watkins in Los Angeles. I hoped that, having underwent surgery once, this would be a simple matter of physical therapy or equipment helping me deal with the lingering pain. I was heartbroken, then, when Dr. Watkins told me that the problem was bigger than that. The first surgery hadn't corrected everything, and I needed to go under the knife again.

"How long will it take me to recover?" I asked quietly.

"Probably several months," Dr. Watkins said. "I'll be honest—it's likely you're going to miss the entire season."

Because it was my second back surgery, I knew right away that my time to recover and rehab was going to be longer than the first time. Dr. Watkins's prognosis was right. It took me until January to get back on the ice. But when I did, things were very different from they had been when I left.

Early into that 2005–06 season, the Blue Jackets had fired our head coach, Gerard Gallant, and hired Ken Hitchcock to replace him. As soon as I returned, Hitchcock singled me out as a veteran, someone he could make an example of for the rest of the team. Before the season, I had been working on my skating with one of our assistant coaches, Gord Murphy. I'd put in extra effort to make sure that I was in the best shape possible. But when Hitchcock arrived, he suggested that I go back to the minors for some conditioning. In private meetings, I pleaded with him to give me a few games to get my timing back and get my feet back under me. We were already out of the playoffs, and I wanted to help out the team however I could. But it was an uphill battle.

As part of my ongoing recovery from the surgeries, I would get extra treatment between periods. The trainers would stretch me and work on me to keep my back loose. One night after getting some more treatment, I was coming back into the locker room to hear what Hitchcock had to say to us before the start of the next period. As I walked down the hallway, he actually gave me the shoulder and bumped into me.

I was so angry I could barely see straight. But luckily, I kept my anger in check.

It wasn't the last time Hitchcock tested my mental strength, either. Late in the season, we had a game against the Rangers at Madison Square Garden. Since we were in New York, a lot of my family came up from Rhode Island to see me play and hang out after the game.

I was looking forward to seeing everyone and to knowing that my family was going to be in the crowd when I stepped on the ice that night. But after the morning skate, I checked the board in the dressing room for the night's lineups, and I didn't see my number up there. Suddenly, I realized: I wasn't in the lineup that night. Hitchcock had made me a healthy scratch. I was gutted and incredibly confused. Why couldn't Hitchcock have told me that the day before? My parents had already driven into town.

Moments like that made it a struggle to motivate myself each day. Each morning, I looked in the mirror and tried to figure out what was staring back at me. I was thirty years old, but I felt twice that age. I had one good eye, and my back was failing me. It took me hours to warm up my body enough for the pain in my back to ease. Any time we took a flight to an away game, I would wait for the seat-belt sign to turn off and then spend as much of the flight walking up and down the aisle as possible. I knew that if I didn't, my back would be a mess the next day.

Each day, on the ice, I could feel my skating style changing, my speed falling a little farther behind the younger guys on the team. No matter how hard I worked during drills or in the gym, it seemed there was nothing I could do to stop the downward slide.

Still, I never complained. I recognized how lucky I was. I still had a place in the NHL, and I was going to earn it and give everything I had for my team.

One morning late in the season, the Red Wings were in town to play us. I was going through some conditioning at the end of our morning skate when I heard my name being called from the bench.

I looked over and Mike Babcock, the Red Wings' coach, was calling me over. I'd never met Babcock in my life, but I skated over to see what he wanted.

"How old are you, Berard?" he asked, leaning over the boards.

"Thirty," I said.

He gave me a look. "And you had two back surgeries? What are you doing? Just retire."

I was about to lay into him when I noticed the smirk on his face and I realized he was joking. "As if!" I said as Babcock chuckled and walked away.

I wasn't ready to stop playing hockey yet, but I could see that my time in Columbus was coming to a close. Hitchcock was making me a healthy scratch more and more often toward the end of the season, and it raised a lot of red flags for me.

After my contract with Columbus expired, Tom had a tough time finding me a new deal for the next season. Funnily enough, the team that ended up taking a chance on me was the same one that had given me my first shot eleven years earlier: the New York Islanders.

Just like in Columbus, I battled all year with the Islanders to try to get my body ready to play. My back was bothering me so much it made it tough. Gerard Gallant had landed with the Islanders as an assistant coach after being fired from Columbus the previous season, and he knew what I could do, so he helped me get ready for each game however he could.

Our head coach that year, Ted Nolan, was a decent guy, but he didn't seem to understand me the way Gallant did. If I made a mistake on the ice, Ted assumed my eye was the problem. At the start of the season, I laughed every time that he said that. Obviously, I can't see out of my right eye, but that didn't affect my game. It was my back that caused me to make misplays or fall a step behind the play. By the end of the season, though, I was sick of hearing about how my eye injury was dragging down the team.

On my thirty-first birthday, in March 2008, I took stock. We were sitting near the bottom of the standings, and I had only dressed for fifty-four games that season. I still wanted to play hockey more than anything, and I felt I still had something to offer. But hockey is a business as much as a game, and I was starting to recognize how the league saw me: as a one-eyed defenseman coming off two back surgeries. A former talent that wasn't worth the risk anymore.

My prospects of playing in the NHL again were slim. I knew the odds were stacked against me. I didn't care, though. My body was trying to tell me I was done playing hockey. But I just wasn't ready to listen just yet.

11

THE KHL

AFTER I WAS DONE PLAYING WITH THE ISLANDERS, I WENT TO THE PHILADEL-phia Flyers' training camp in the fall of 2008. The Flyers' general manager, Paul Holmgren, and I always had a good relationship, and he was in Philly at the time. He brought me in, and I felt that I had a good camp. I was convinced I could make the team as their fourth or fifth defenseman.

On the very last day of camp, Paul called me in the office.

"Bryan, thanks for coming in," Paul said.

"No trouble," I said. "I'm excited for the season."

"About that," Paul said. "We have a young defenseman, Luca Sbisa, and we want to give him a shot at making the team this year. I know you can still play, but at your age, we felt it was best for the team to go with the younger player."

His words hit me like a ton of bricks. *I'm not that old*, I thought.

But I took a breath to steady myself. "Thanks for letting me know, Paul," I said, my voice breaking a bit. "I'm disappointed. I really felt I could have brought something to the team."

We shook hands and I slowly pushed myself out of my chair. I respected Paul for being honest and straightforward, but I was in shock. Walking out of Paul's office, I knew my NHL career was over.

I wasn't done playing hockey, so I went home and thought about my options.

I'd finished my repayments to the insurance companies, and with the investments that I had with Phil and elsewhere, I thought I had built myself a pretty good financial nest egg. Still, the competitive spirit lodged deep within me meant that I wasn't ready to stop playing hockey yet. *Maybe there's another option*, I thought.

I called my agent to talk it through. I had left Tom Laidlaw and taken on Paul Theofanous as my agent. Paul was based out of New York, and among his many talents, one was his ability to speak fluent Russian.

"How would you feel about playing in Russia?" Paul asked when I filled him in on the situation.

"Honestly, it's never crossed my mind until right now," I said.

"It can be a bit of a crapshoot," Paul said. "But let me talk to my contacts and see what I can do."

A few days later, Paul called me back with an offer. Vityaz Chekhov, a team based out of Podolsk, an industrial city an hour south of Moscow, had offered me a deal. I couldn't have placed Podolsk on a map, but I was in. The money was right, and it gave me a chance to keep playing professional hockey at a high level.

"What the heck?" I said when Paul outlined the deal. "Let's do it."

It was a whirlwind getting ready for the move. Luckily, I was going to have some company. A buddy of mine and former NHLer, Chris Simon, was going to be playing on the same team as me. I didn't know much about Russia, but I recognized that this wasn't going to be the same as hopping from New York to Boston—this was going to be like going to a different world.

But the craziest part of the trip came before I even left. A few weeks before I headed to Russia, I got a call from the FBI. *Why is the FBI calling me?* I thought when I answered the call. A couple of special agents asked if we could meet the next day.

"We'd like to speak to you about your dealings with Phil Kenner," one of the agents said.

The next day, I met with Special Agent Matt Galioto and another agent. I didn't know what the meeting was about or what they wanted with Phil. They didn't present any evidence or accusations—I got the sense they were just feeling me out, trying to see exactly what my relationship with Phil was like and how he handled my money. I answered whatever questions they had and tried to be helpful, even though I didn't really know what they were looking for.

A few hours later, the agents headed on their way.

"We'll be in touch," one of them said.

I headed home, trying to process what had just happened. I had more questions than answers, but one thing was clear: something was going on, and it wasn't good.

•   •   •

Paul flew over to Russia with Chris and me to introduce us to the team's owner, Nikolai. When we arrived after our nine-hour flight from NYC, my first impression of the town was pretty grim. I expected to find a Russia in early winter that was covered in pristine snow. But as I stared out of the car window, all of the snow along the roadside was black from pollution. All of the apartment buildings looked the same, too—big, cement compounds that looked like carbon copies of each other.

We pulled up in front of a hotel in downtown Podolsk. It wasn't a nice hotel at all—in fact, it was worse than the cheapest hotels I'd seen back home.

After we settled in, Nikolai came by to meet us for dinner and drinks. Nikolai didn't speak English, but he had some bodyguards who did, and they and Paul translated for us all. We quickly discovered that Nikolai was a big drinker, and the next thing I knew, it was after three in the morning.

Between the meal and the jet lag, I was exhausted. I asked Paul to tell Nikolai thanks for his generosity, but that I needed to get some sleep. I had my first practice the next day, so I needed a little bit of rest.

I went back to my room and had just fallen asleep when I heard a huge pounding on my door. It really startled me, and I woke up right away. I looked out and saw it was Paul, my agent. I told him that I was exhausted and to leave me alone. He didn't budge, he just told me to open the door right away.

I opened the door, and there were hot-looking women standing next to Nikolai. He looked at me and said a few words in Russian. Paul translated, "Nikolai says, welcome to the team."

I didn't know what to say, so I looked at the girls and said, "All right, come on in." And that was my formal introduction to life in the KHL.

I quickly discovered that life in the KHL was like living in the Wild West. A couple of days after arriving in town, we drove by a car accident and there was a dead body lying by the side of the road. It wasn't covered up—the body was just lying there. It freaked me out when I saw that.

Thankfully, I never felt as though we were in any trouble or any danger. The team always made sure we had bodyguards and drivers, so we were well protected.

As part of our welcome to Russia, Nikolai invited a bunch of the players on the team over to his place. This wasn't a modest dinner or anything like that, though. Nikolai had a fifty-acre compound that was filled with armed guards.

Once you entered the compound, the first thing I saw was that he had exotic animals of all sorts on display. One of the guys on the team mentioned that Nikolai even had a wild wolf that lived in a fenced-in compound within the property. I could believe it. I knew that Nikolai bred big dogs—I'm not sure what kind they were, but they must have weighed at least 150 pounds. He offered to give me and Chris a puppy to take home with us. We politely declined.

We walked inside the house, and there was every kind of wine you could think of for us to choose from.

Everything seemed over the top. Nikolai had a classic Russian sauna that was built of mahogany. When you walked into it, you felt as though you were in a James Bond movie. There were beds made of marble with woodstoves underneath them to heat the stone, and piles of real polar bear fur rugs. Some guys would wrap themselves in the rugs and lie down on the heated bed for a nap, while others threw the furs around their shoulders as they walked around the compound, smoking and talking.

In all my years in the NHL, I had never seen or even heard of anything as outrageous as Nikolai and his compound. *What have I got myself into?* I thought.

Nikolai was generous to his players, but if he didn't trust you, it was immediately clear.

My teammate in the KHL, Chris Simon, was also a client of Phil Kenner. One night early in the season, the two of us started talking about our experiences with Phil, and our stories weren't matching up. Later that night, I looked back through my emails with Phil, and I started to notice suspicious lines and dodges that I hadn't seen before. My meeting with the FBI was still fresh in my mind. I was starting to wonder just what the hell was going on with Kenner and his financial dealings.

Through all of this, Phil was still trying to get more money from me and Chris. He even flew all the way to Russia to meet with us. He said there was a new investment opportunity he wanted to talk about in person.

Phil showed up at the hotel that was owned by Nikolai, who happened to be there when we were meeting Phil. From the second he saw him, Nikolai did not like the way Phil looked.

Nikolai called me and Chris into his office the day after we met with Phil at the hotel.

"I don't like the look of him," Nikolai said. "I don't like the way he dresses." Phil looked more like a surfer than a financial advisor to Nikolai, and his street smarts kicked in. You didn't last long in the highest levels of business in Russia without getting a master's degree in street smarts.

To us hockey players, we didn't care how Phil dressed. We just figured that's how he was and how he dressed. But the experience was enough to spook Phil. He stayed in his hotel room for two days before taking off back to the United States. I still had lingering questions and doubts. I told myself I'd figure it all out when I got back to the United States. For now, though, there was still hockey ahead.

•   •   •

As crazy as life off the ice was proving to be in Russia, the actual games in the KHL were very skilled. The top-two lines for all the teams in the KHL were filled with guys who had played in the NHL, or who had the talent to play there. On defense, then, I had to be sharp. We played a lot more zone defense than I was used to, so I was learning new systems and skills every day.

The main difference, though, was that games in the KHL were played on the bigger, Olympic-sized ice. I loved the bigger ice, as it worked well with my style of play. It gave me more time and space to move the puck and make plays offensively, and there was a lot less hitting, so I wasn't as worried about my eye.

Jaromir Jagr was playing for Avangard Omsk when I went over to play in the KHL. I'd seen firsthand that Jaromir Jagr was great in the NHL, but somehow he was even better in the KHL. With his skill on that big ice surface, he was almost unstoppable. When he had the puck down low, he was so strong; you couldn't take the puck off him. As a defenseman, all you could do was let Jagr do his thing and hope that you could cover the other guys that he was trying to pass the puck to.

Before I headed to Russia, I had heard the KHL wasn't as rough as the NHL. I quickly discovered that was the furthest thing from the truth. Those Russian guys loved to fight. Chris suffered from it more than I did. The younger Russian players were always trying to pick on him. Chris was six feet, three inches tall and weighed well over 220 pounds. He was a big, scary player.

A lot of the time, it seemed to me that the opposing coaches were trying to get the younger Russian players to test Chris. Chris tried to remain patient. Most of the time, he'd just shrug them off and say, "Guys, I am not here to fight." Chris played with me on the power play, and he had great hands. He scored 144 goals in the NHL—I don't care how tough you are, you need to have some skill to score that many goals in the NHL. All Chris wanted to do in the KHL was play the game, score goals, and make some money.

But game after game, these young players would stay on Chris, running him and taunting him until he snapped. And when that happened, those younger players regretted it. I loved Chris, but if he got angry, he would go into this other world when he was fighting. Chris would be dominating in a fight, and when it was clear it was over, I would have to start yelling at Chris to let the other guy go. It would take me a few times screaming his name before Chris came to his senses.

I fought more in my twenty-five-game stint in the KHL than I did in any NHL season.

I ended up getting into five fights throughout the season, and I got beat up in three of them. Most times, it was the same story: the other team's tough guy would try to fight Chris, and Chris would end up beating the other guy. That would start a line brawl and the tough guy whom Chris beat up would get back up from where Chris left him, pissed off and ready to take it out on me.

I ended up with 103 penalty minutes in only twenty-five games in the KHL. In my entire NHL career, I never had a season where I had more than 100 PIMs. That year, I had 103 penalty minutes in twenty-five games. Chris ended up with 263 PIMs.

I gradually came to see that, as good as life was for the players, a darker reality lurked beneath the surface. Just before I joined the team, Vitayz were playing Jaromir Jagr's team when one of his teammates, Alexei Cherepanov, a Rangers prospect, collapsed on the bench. For a while, it was all the guys on the team could talk about when I joined the team. They had never seen anything like it and a lot them were, understandably, still rattled from the incident.

I was told that the game immediately came to a halt while the trainers started trying to resuscitate Cherepanov. People kept screaming for the paramedics and ambulance that were supposed to be at the rink. But there were only five minutes left in the game, and the ambulance had left the rink early because the paramedics wanted to beat the traffic.

While the ambulance tried to get back to the arena, somebody grabbed the defibrillator and hooked it up to Cherepanov. But when they tried to turn it on, they found the machine was dead.

Eventually, the guys were sent back to our locker room. A little while later, they were told the news—Cherepanov had died on the bench. The poor kid was only nineteen years old.

Apparently, Nikolai snapped after that. He wanted to go after the paramedics and hold them responsible. There were a lot of questions surrounding Cherepanov's death—about the paramedics, the defibrillator, his health conditions. It was a chilling reminder of just how far away from home I was.

When we had some time off and needed to escape the pressure and confinement of Podolsk, Chris and I would take a trip into Moscow.

We would meet up with other North American guys playing in the area, like Ray Emery. Ray Emery was well liked by everyone. I never played with Razor, but you could just tell he was a good team guy.

Moscow was an expensive city, and a metropolitan one filled with an incredible amount of history. We would stay in a nice hotel for a night or two, go out for meals and drinks, and live the high life for a little while. It didn't cost much to live like kings. But then we'd return to Podolsk, where I saw the contrast between the poverty of the industrial cities compared to the money flowing through the capital. It always rubbed me the wrong way. I'd grown up closer to Podolsk than the bright lights of Moscow, and no matter how much I enjoyed the scene, I always reminded myself to remain humble.

We got to see a lot of Russia throughout that year. Of course, that meant that there was a lot of travel involved. I had never been scared of flying before coming to Russia, but the flights on our team plane changed my mind. The first time I boarded it, I stopped in my tracks. There were two rows of two seats along the length of the plane. The cargo hold wasn't big enough to fit all of our equipment, either. Players in Russia are responsible for their own bags and laundry, so as we boarded, each guy would take their turn dumping their stinky bag into one of the back seats in a giant pile. Every time that we took off, I was convinced the plane would be too tail-heavy to make it off the ground.

The seats were small and uncomfortable, which was ruinous for my back. No matter how I tried to position myself, I was always in some level of pain. The teams in the KHL were spread all across the country, which meant that sometimes a road game was a nine-hour flight away. Sometimes we would fly overnight and land at six in the morning and we had to be ready to go for that night.

What was more alarming, though, was when I discovered they didn't deice the planes in Russia.

On one of our first flights, I looked out the window before we took off.

"Who are those guys with the brooms under the wings?" I asked my teammate beside me.

He peered out the window. "That's the ground crew deicing the plane," he said.

The dressing rooms had the same kind of do-it-yourself, manual style. In a lot of rinks across the league, when you wanted to take a shower, you had to let the water run for at least thirty minutes, because the water would come out black for the first half hour.

A lot of the toilets over there wouldn't let you flush toilet paper, either, which meant that the toilet paper went in the garbage. Needless to say, going to the bathroom at the rink took a lot of guts.

Thankfully, Chris and I had a nice home to retreat to. The team had put us up in a cabin-style house at the edge of Podolsk, near the surrounding countryside. It was so remote that, at night, we could hear the wild dogs howling from the nearby forest.

The team gave us a car, too, and a personal driver/bodyguard. He was a young guy who had scars all along his forearms from getting into knife fights when he was in jail. Our driver carried a knife and a gun at all times. He used to say the gun was the backup.

The second night we were in the house, Chris and I were watching TV when we heard a knock at the door. We answered it nervously, but we were relieved to see it was our driver. He walked over to the kitchen island and put down a Glock 9mm pistol and a box of ammunition.

"For you," he said.

Chris and I looked at each other, our eyebrows raised.

Our driver looked at our faces. "It's for your safety," he said. "Don't worry, they're rubber-tipped bullets. They'll hurt, but they won't kill anyone."

He explained that if anyone ever came to the house late at night, we should call him right away.

"But first," he said, "shoot them. Then call me."

Thankfully, we never had to use the gun. Some of the other tips he had for us, though—like always carry American cash on you—proved to be incredibly helpful.

One weekend, I was headed into Moscow to meet up with Ray Emery and some of the other former NHLers. I had learned that there was no such thing as lanes in Russia—people drove at top speed everywhere, and on a three-lane highway, there could be six or seven lanes of traffic. It was survival of the fittest.

Nikolai and our driver/bodyguard had both told us that if we ever got into an accident, we should pay the other person in cash and get out of there. "Never, ever wait for the cops to arrive," our driver said ominously.

That weekend, I was trying to change lanes when I hit another car. Both of our vehicles were a little banged up. We pulled over to the side of the road and inspected the damage. I didn't speak enough Russian to talk to the other guy, but I took out $1,000 in American bills and gave it to the other driver. His eyes went wide, and he grabbed the money, hustled back to his car, and got out of there. I quickly did the same thing.

It helped that playing in the KHL, we got paid in cash. I got paid four times while I was in the KHL. Each payday, we would get called to the rink and head upstairs to the office. We would sign the logbook, proving we picked up our payment, and then the team official would hand us a bag of cash. It was the same thing every time. The only difference was what currency we got paid in. My first payday, I was paid in U.S. dollars. The next time, it was euros. Then Russian rubles, and then U.S. dollars again.

As soon as we signed for our payment, our driver would take us straight to a government-run bank. We'd been warned to only use the state banks. Chris first decided to open an account with a private bank he found near the arena. He deposited money in it, but partway through the season, he showed up and discovered the bank had gone out of business without any notice. All of the money he'd deposited was gone.

I felt bad for Chris, but I was glad I'd gone with the government bank. Still, it had its drawbacks. In order to make sure my money was safely transferred back to my accounts in America, I had to take the money to a teller. The teller would then go through each individual bill in the cash I was depositing to make sure the amount was correct and that it wasn't counterfeit. Only then would they initiate the wire transfer back to America. The whole process usually took up to four hours, but I felt better knowing that it was in a safe place. Or so I thought.

• • •

After my season in Vityaz Chekhov, I headed back to the United States to recharge and visit with family and friends. Over the summer, I debated my options. Playing in the KHL had been wild, but I wasn't sure if I was going to go back for another year. If I did, I at least wanted to play for a different team.

Alexander Mogilny had reached out to me to see if I was interested in going back to play in the KHL. Mogilny grew up in a town called Amur, just east of Siberia, close to the Chinese border. Amur had a KHL team in the KHL, and Mogilny, who was the part owner and GM of the team at the time, was wondering if I was interested in signing there, too.

After talking to Mogilny, I weighed my options. Most contracts in the KHL for North American players are for one-year terms, and they're not guaranteed—if the team wants to fire you and not pay you, they can do it just about anytime they want.

Ultimately, I decided that I would play in Amur for my second season in the KHL. Despite the concerns, I wanted to keep playing hockey, and I needed to keep making money.

So, I headed back to Russia in the fall, and I got there in better shape than I was the year before. I took my physicals and medicals, and I was ready to report to the team, when suddenly, I got a notice from the KHL that I hadn't passed my physical. The official report was that I had failed my physical because of my elevated liver enzymes.

I couldn't understand it. I do have hereditary elevated levels, but I'd been fine to play in the NHL with my fatty liver, and it hadn't gotten any worse. And the year before, there hadn't been any issues with my physical. If anything, I was healthier now than I had been before. What was the problem?

I never figured out exactly why I'd failed my physical. I heard rumors that some owners in the league could get unhappy when their players moved elsewhere, and so they'd block them from signing with their competitors. I wasn't sure if that was the case, but one thing was clear: I had no future in the KHL.

I stayed in Amur for a week, trying to get my medical sorted out.

Mogilny kept reassuring me, saying that the whole thing was ridiculous and that I shouldn't worry. I was tested again, and the league doctors wouldn't clear me. I then flew into Moscow to do a series of tests with other doctors. Same results. I even went back to New York and saw a series of specialists. All of them passed me and said I should be cleared to play. They even wrote an official letter to the KHL, informing them that I was in perfect health.

I took the letter and test results back to Moscow to see the KHL doctors. They tested me once more, and they failed me again. No matter what I did, it seemed the KHL doctors would not clear me to play.

It dawned on me that this was the end of my professional hockey career. It wasn't the glorious exit I'd imagined, with me hoisting the Cup and going out on a winning note. No, the end of my playing days came in a nondescript Russian doctor's office, with a piece of paper crumpled in my fist.

So many thoughts raced through my head, but one question kept coming up over and over: What was I going to do with the rest of my life? I had to head back to the United States; that much was obvious. But beyond that? I had no clue.

On the flight home, I tried to console myself. I had lots of experience behind me and time ahead to work with. I had my family, friends, and health—all of the most important things. I didn't know *what* I was going to do, but I knew *how* I was going to figure it out, the same way I always had: by picking myself up and steeling myself for whatever came next. My mom's words came back to me: "'Never' does not exist in our family's vocabulary." They were words I would need in the days to come.

12

FRAUD AND FORGERY

WHEN I RETURNED FROM PLAYING IN RUSSIA, I MOVED BACK TO NEW YORK City. I didn't have a job lined up, and I didn't know what I was going to do. I also didn't know what I was going to do to earn money. What I should have been worrying about, though, was how to keep the money I'd already earned.

Only a few weeks after I returned, I was contacted by the FBI again. Special Agents Scott Romanowski and Matt Galioto brought me into their office in the Southern District of New York. I spent hours with them, answering questions and going over a bunch of paperwork.

I still had little clue what was going on. Every time I could get a word in, I asked them if they could tell me why I was there, what Phil had done wrong, or whether I was in trouble. They didn't give away much, and they always just steered me back to whatever question they had for me.

I kept reaching out to the agents over the coming months, pleading with them to shed some light on what was happening and what I should do about it.

Finally, the agents brought me back into their office. They sat me down and put a piece of paper in front me.

"Did you approve all the money spent in this line of credit?" they asked.

I knew that Kenner was opening up lines of credit in my name. He'd done the same thing for other players whose money he was handling. Kenner told us that the bank needed it, but that he was never going to touch the line of credit himself or use the money in it. But based on the documents the agents were showing me, Kenner had been forging my signature for the bank and spending the money in my line of credit at will.

"What are you talking about?" I asked. "I didn't know anyone was spending money in my line of credit."

They pulled out another document. "How about this land sale in Hawaii? Do you remember approving that?"

"No," I said. "I invested in it. What do you mean it was sold?" Years before, I had owned an H1 Hummer, an amazing vehicle that I'd loved. I bought it for $110,000, and I owned it for three years. The book value on the vehicle by that point was $68,000. I'd sold it to the investment corporation that Phil had set up, with the understanding that the company would ship the car to Hawaii so that we could use it to visit potential investment properties. But the agents showed me that instead of buying the car through the corporation's accounts, Phil had dipped into my personal line of credit to buy it and then gifted the car to his own company. I'd effectively bought my own car twice.

As I looked through the bank statements the agents were showing me, I felt myself start to sweat.

"Do you remember spending any of the money from your lines of credit?" one agent asked.

"I told you, that money was never supposed to be touched," I said quietly. "I was told I needed it to give to the bank."

Over the next few hours, Matt and his partner showed me a series of financial transactions. Every single one of them was in my name, and I never gave permission for or authorized any of them. There was a notarized document that had my signature on it and that was signed in Scottsdale, Arizona. But on the date that was listed on the paperwork, I was playing in an NHL game in Buffalo.

I discovered that Phil had been buying property for years under his name, using my savings and a line of credit he had opened up in my name, one that I never knew about. When I was in the NHL, Kenner sometimes visited me and other clients in the league on the road. He would have us sign a whole bunch of documents and papers, telling us it was regular upkeep for our investment portfolios. What we didn't realize was that Kenner was taking those signatures and opening up phony lines of credit. He would go to a bank, and use the bonds and savings we entrusted to him as collateral against the line of credit. When the line of credit defaulted, he then used the money in the savings to pay off the maxed-out line of credit.

The more information the agents showed me, the more I realized how much I'd been ripped off. Phil had been double-dipping, and I'd had no idea what was happening. The total was staggering—he'd opened up $700,000 in fraudulent lines of credit under my name.

I was fuming, but at the same time I was scared. I immediately realized all this money—money I had earned and put away over de-cades—was gone.

I had a bit of spare cash in my bank accounts, but other than that, I had nothing to show for all of my years in the NHL. All of those long road trips, the hours spent training and competing. All of it was for nothing. I was broke.

I didn't know what to do and where to turn. I struggled to wrap my head around the financial damage, but I was also gutted personally. I had considered Phil to be more than just my financial advisor. He had become a close friend. After Phil went through a divorce, he spent two Christmases with my family at our house. Phil acted like he was one of our teammates—it's what had made me trust him in the first place. And, looking back, it's probably what had made my mom so wary, too.

In the days following my meeting with the FBI agents, I tried to make sense of everything. Ever since the conversations Chris and I had in Russia, and given the inconsistencies in what we were each hearing from Phil, I knew something wasn't quite right with our investments. But it was 2008, and the stock market had just crashed. The major-ity of the loans for our real estate deals had been negotiated with the Lehman Brothers. When the real estate market in the United States crashed, Lehman Brothers went bankrupt, and our deals were voided.

The problems we were seeing in our personal bank accounts, then, seemed to be easily explained by a downturn in the overall market. I'd never had serious reason to doubt Phil's word, and honestly, I didn't have the technical knowledge or expertise to look deeper into what was going on with my investments. As far as I could tell, Phil had always been doing everything by the book.

I'd done my due diligence, too. Or at least, I thought I had. I was one of the few clients Phil had who went to every single property that we were going to invest in. Other guys just sent Phil the money he was asking for. But I made sure to get on a plane and visit them all. The real estate market had been hot at the time, and my real estate ventures was supposed to be my post-hockey career—one that would keep me and my family financially secure for years to come. I needed to make sure they were the real deal.

So I went to see all of the properties. I traveled to ones south of San Diego, and in Cabo San Lucas, Mexico. I went to Hawaii, and I went to the east cape of the Baja region of Mexico. Every time, there was a development happening. And a lot of the properties were very beautiful. When I saw them—seaside locales in tropical regions—I could see how they would be worth an investment and produce money for years to come. One of the properties—the one in Hawaii—even had a coffee field. I thought ruefully about how, in a better world, I could have been there, producing high-end coffee right now, instead of trying to figure out how to piece my life back together.

The more I went back over events, the more I realized how naïve I'd been. I was angry—at Phil, at the system that had allowed those investments to happen. But most of all, I was angry at myself.

I talked to some of the other players who had been involved with Kenner, trying to see if we could make some sense of things through our shared experiences. Through those connections, I got back in touch with John Kaiser, a former New York cop.

I first met John through Phil in early 2003. He was a cop by day, but in his spare time, he built homes and flipped them. He was a street-smart guy, and he was easy to get along with, and we hit it off right away.

Kenner had left some boxes with John and at first, John thought they had something to do with a real estate deal he was a part of in Hermosa Beach, California. But when the accusations against Kenner started swirling, John went through the documents more closely. Bit by bit, he was able to piece everything together.

John contacted me, and we started to go over our notes. It was then that we realized just how bad it was. John and I drove to Buffalo to speak with some other players and collect any evidence we could from them, all of which we promptly passed along to the FBI to help with their investigation. After that trip to Buffalo, John and I were in contact with the FBI almost daily, going over any and all evidence that we could find.

I should have seen the warning signs. I had often visited Phil at his house in Scottsdale when I was playing in the NHL. Anytime we were hanging out, if a client called, the first thing Phil would say was, "I'll call you right back." He'd excuse himself, then go pick up his laptop and head to his office, where he'd grab an external hard drive. He had a separate one for each NHL player he worked with. He'd connect the hard drive to his laptop, head to a different room, and continue the conversation in private.

At the time, I thought it was professional, as though Phil were respecting our privacy. Looking back on it, though, I had to wonder if it was his way of making sure none of us could compare our accounts and to keep everything hidden.

A lot of our financial mail was going to his house directly, too. Some of it we knew about and he'd forward to us. Other pieces of it, we never knew existed. Our statements for our bond portfolios, for example, went directly to his home in Scottsdale. One of Kenner's friends later confided in me that they were burning a lot of those statements in the backyard fire pit.

I also realized I should have listened more. Phil had a secretary who had previously tried to blow the whistle and quietly warn Phil's clients about what was happening. She was one of the first whistle-blowers. In hindsight, I could see she had been right, and I really wish I had listened to her at the time. Some of the smarter guys did, and they got out. But others, well, Phil had brainwashed us, and we either couldn't hear what the secretary had to say, or we didn't want to hear it. The result was a lot of hard feelings and burnt bridges, and I felt worse about the personal losses than I did about the financial ones.

•   •   •

When the FBI finally arrested Phil, they got him at the gym.

It was 2013, and the FBI had staked out the gym where Kenner worked out. They waited until he went in and started working out. During the middle of Kenner's workout, the FBI walked into the gym, surrounded him, and arrested him in the predawn hours.

After all the people that he hurt and all the money that was lost, it felt great to hear that Kenner had been arrested. I only wish I could have been there to see the look on his face when the FBI led him away in handcuffs.

Before Kenner's hearing, a court officer came up to me and asked if I wanted to see Kenner behind bars at the courthouse. Tommy Constantine, Kenner's business partner and accomplice—he'd opened up a phony prepaid credit card company called Eufora, which Kenner used to move around his money and hide it from the authorities—was in jail with him.

"Am I allowed?" I asked.

The marshal frowned. "Kenner defrauded some cops out of their life savings," he said. "I'm heading down now. I can take you down, if you want."

"Lead the way," I said.

The marshal brought me down to the holding cell, where I finally saw Kenner and Constantine behind bars. I hated them both, but Kenner had done the most damage to me. Looking at Phil sitting in that holding cell, knowing everything he did to me and everyone else and all the money that people lost to fraud, I felt some small measure of satisfaction knowing that justice was being served.

I was lucky compared to many other people that Phil hurt. I was a single guy, and the only person who was hurt was me. I felt awful when I thought about the people who had kids to take care of who'd lost all of their savings. The thought of what they were going through was sickening.

I never really understood the concept of credit scores and ratings. When I broke into the NHL, I was young and naïve. I let bills pile up over weeks and months, and then I'd pick a Sunday afternoon to sit down and write checks to pay them all. I had the money to pay the bills, and I didn't think there was anything wrong if I did so a few days late.

I should have known. When I was growing up in Woonsocket, I had watched my mom sit down to pay the bills each month. She counted every penny, meticulously checking what they'd made at the garage with what was in the checkbook. My family never made a lot of money, but I'd never wanted for anything, and my parents always paid the bills on time.

Now, as I restarted my finances, the idea of a credit score was all-important to me. I had a little bit of money left over from my play-ing days in my 401(k). But it was clear that, for the foreseeable future, I'd be living month to month. I needed to find work to pay the bills.

Thankfully, in 2014, I met Brad Dorman, one of the managing partners at a wealth management company called Whale Rock Point Partners, and things started to look a little brighter. Brad offered me a job with the company. I would work closely with Tyson Reed, the COO of the company. Tyson and his team would handle the nuts and bolts of the investment portfolios. My job was to develop new clients.

I immediately took to the new job and I loved working there. I quickly started to see parallels between my hockey career and my new job. When I played, I loved carrying the puck up the ice and making a play for a teammate. I was doing the same thing with Tyson and his team, but instead of passing the puck, I was passing along clients to pros in the office who would take care of their money.

Seeing the care that Tyson and his team put into their work made me proud to work alongside them. More than once I found myself wishing I'd met them before Phil Kenner!

After the court case, I did my best to put all of what happened with Phil into the rearview mirror and move on. I had learned the hard way that money could ruin the best friendships in the world. I could earn back my savings, but I could never regain the friendships I lost.

But as angry as everything made me, what was done was done. I recognized that I couldn't change what happened. So I did what I always do when life knocked me down—I picked myself up and kept going.

13

MIND OVER BODY

FOR A LONG TIME AFTER MY PROFESSIONAL HOCKEY CAREER ENDED, I WAS angry. The loss of my life savings and betrayal by Phil had left a bitter taste in my mouth. Each day, I would work myself into a foul mood, and then I'd head out in the evening for a few beers to try to unwind. A couple of hours later, I'd still be stewing, ready to fight anyone who crossed me.

I realized I couldn't keep going like this. It was too painful, too toxic. I wanted to get my life back on track and focus on my future, but I couldn't do that if I was unable to let go of the past.

My friends and family noticed that something wasn't right. They could tell I wasn't my usual self. My family and I had done some family counseling for my younger brother, Bruce, to help him get through some of the mental health struggles he faced. I'd seen firsthand the impact that the simple act of reaching out for help could have.

I needed to talk to someone about my anger management and have them help me figure out how to process and navigate my transition into a new life. So I reached out to Dr. Shaw and Dr. Lewis from the NHLPA to see if they could get me the help I needed. Dr. Shaw referred me to this therapist in New York City, and I immediately started regular sessions with her.

Nobody should be ashamed about talking to a therapist and getting the help that they need. When you play in the NHL, you can often take out your frustrations on the ice during the game. Once you retire from the NHL, though, that option is gone. You've entered a different world. The frustrations might still be there, so you need to find ways to deal with them in a healthy manner.

My first few meetings with the therapist were revelatory. Talking to her, I realized how much I still had to process and resolve following my eye injury. I had been so focused on getting back to the NHL and on making up for what I had lost that I had never stopped to reflect on and acknowledge what had happened.

My parents had always taught me that if you had something to say, you should say it in a respectful manner. Along the way, my anger had clouded that lesson, but I was finally returning to it. *If only I'd talked to a therapist years ago*, I thought. I remembered all of the times when I should have kept my mouth shut, or when I lost my temper. I wish I'd acted differently or managed those situations more maturely.

I acknowledged what I'd done, but with my therapist's help, I didn't let myself wallow in guilt. As the weeks and months passed, I began to have more good days than bad. My habits and responses began to change. My parents visited me one weekend, and as I was showing them around my apartment, my mom gave me a funny look.

"You've become a clean freak in your old age," she teased.

She was right. When I was playing in the NHL, I would let messes pile up. But since I stopped playing hockey and started working with my therapist, my habits had started to change. I liked things done a certain way, and I was always cleaning or washing my place to keep it in order. It was like a mild form of OCD, even if it didn't come with an official diagnosis. I would be at a friend's place for a party, and after the guests left, I'd still be there, wiping down counters and washing dishes. My friends joked that they'd invite me to all of their parties if they knew I'd clean the entire house after.

I was finally feeling like I was in a steadier place in my life. My inner battles had quieted down, and I slowly started to think about what other new experiences I might explore.

The answer came in the form of a phone call in 2011. The producers of the TV show *Battle of the Blades* were wondering if I was interested in being a contestant on the show.

At first, I was hesitant. I was out of shape, and my life was centered in New York City, while the show filmed in Toronto. And I'd never worn a pair of figure skates in my life—I was afraid I'd make a fool of myself. I told the producers I would think about it, and I figured they would move on.

But they kept calling me, week after week, urging me to come to Toronto and meet everyone involved in the production. I finally caved and agreed, and I was glad I did. As I toured the set and talked to the people working on the show, I discovered that there was a charity angle to it that I'd never known about. Each pair of skaters on the show represents a charity of their choice. The better their place in the competition, the more money they make for their charity.

I was in. This wasn't just a game show—it was a chance to raise awareness and money for a good cause. My first thought was that I would take part in the show to support a charity working with blind children. But after I signed on to the show, the wife of one of my ex-teammates reached out to me and told me about some recent tragic news. Luke Richardson, a former NHL player, and his wife, Stephanie, had just created a charity called the Do-It-for-Daron Foundation. Their daughter, Daron, had committed suicide the year before at just fourteen years old. Luke and Stephanie had founded the charity for mental health awareness and suicide prevention. My former teammate's wife asked if I might consider supporting Daron's charity.

I thought about my brother, Bruce, and the demons he'd fought, and I reflected on the help that my therapist had given me in dealing with my own mental health issues. I knew what I had to do.

I contacted Luke and Stephanie, and I asked them if it was okay if I made the Do-It-for-Daron Foundation my charity on *Battle of the Blades*. I was thrilled when they said yes, and I was determined to do well in the competition to help them in any way that I could.

And it really was a competition. We were on the ice anywhere from four to six hours a day, and the coaches pushed us hard. I immediately had a newfound appreciation for figure skaters. I was partnered with Marie-France Dubreuil, who had competed at several Olympics and world championships. She and her husband, Patrice Lauzon, were some of the best skaters I had ever seen. I watched how they used the edges of their skates and positioned their bodies to glide across the ice while entertaining and performing along the way, making it look effortless the entire time. *If I ever have a kid who wants to play hockey, they're learning on figure skates first*, I thought.

It helped having other NHL alumni, like Brad May and Wade Belak, be a part of the show. I had been friends with them before we started competing against each other on the show, so each practice felt like a mini-reunion. We would meet every morning in the hotel restaurant for breakfast. Other skaters would join us, and there was usually at least six of us there grabbing something to eat. Wade was always among them, smiling and chatting while we ate. Afterward, we'd head to our respective rooms to rest, grab our things, and then head to the rink for practice later in the day.

On the afternoon of August 31, 2011, I showed up at the rink for practice as usual. We were all out on the ice, warming up for the day's practice, when one of the producers called us over. As I got closer, I could see that there were tears in his eyes.

"I have some terrible news," the producer said. "Wade has died."

The producer shared that Wade had committed suicide, and we all immediately broke into tears. I was devastated. Even after everything I'd seen in my family and been through myself, I wasn't prepared to lose a friend. Not like that. The bit of understanding I had about mental illness didn't make it any easier. You can understand that mental illness affects so many people around the world, but when it hits home, it's next to impossible to wrap your head around it. I couldn't imagine what his family was going through.

The news about Wade was heart-wrenching for everyone involved with the show. The entire cast and crew did their best to rally together, trying to do justice to Wade's memory. We dedicated the show to him, but there was a lingering sense of sorrow throughout the entire season. Marie-France and I placed second, and I was extra glad that the money we'd raised was going to such a worthy cause.

I suffered anywhere from three to five concussions during my NHL career. Every now and then, I would get the pins-and-needles feeling in my arm that sometimes comes with lasting nerve damage as a result of a concussion. But most of the lingering pain I had was from my back and my eye. The pain I felt and the injuries I had were describable, and there was no stigma attached to them.

I couldn't imagine the sorts of scars Wade was carrying. I had a wide range of reactions in the weeks that followed—grief at losing my friend, anger at the lack of support for his health issues, fear for what other mental health issues lurked among other alumni. I had seen other friends throughout the league suffer in silence. I'd witnessed the changes in their demeanor, their depression, their migraines. It never got easier to see.

•   •   •

The hockey world seems big, but in many ways it's a small community. I miss joking around with the guys, pranking and teasing each other while we were in the dressing room and getting ready to play. Those moments spent sitting in the dressing room, when you and your team-mates are chirping each other and having a laugh while you get ready, were priceless. But of all the things I miss about playing in the NHL, the camaraderie is what I miss the most.

As I entered a new phase in my life, I realized one thing above all else: it's the people in our life that make it worth living. In the years after my retirement, I went to a number of alumni events. Every single one was a blast. When all the retired players got together and sat around a table after a function or a banquet, none of us wanted to go to bed. We had a phrase for it—MOS, or Missing Out Syndrome, our private version of FOMO, or fear of missing out. Nobody wanted to miss anything, so we would stay up late and tell more stories.

Sometimes, sitting at the table with the other alumni, I'd look around and wonder how my life might have been different if my career hadn't been cut short by my eye injury. What sort of person would I have become? Could I have helped a team win a Stanley Cup? How long could I have played?

In hindsight, I didn't have any regrets about coming back from my eye injury. If I had to do it all over again, I would have done the exact same thing. Making a comeback to hockey gave me that many more years of stories, of friends, of chances to follow my dream. I lost an eye, but I gained a whole new lease on life in the process.

I would always wonder what could have been, but those thoughts were outweighed by the gratitude I felt for the many good things I had in my life. I had no regrets about my playing career. I always played hard, and I looked forward to stepping onto the ice every night. No matter what mistakes I made or setbacks I encountered, I picked myself up and moved on to the next shift. It's not how you fall that defines who you are—it's how you pick yourself up and keep going to make yourself the best person you can be. I didn't know what life was going to bring next for me. But after everything I'd seen in my life, I was ready to go wherever the road might take me.

EPILOGUE

NOT LONG AGO, I WAS HANGING OUT WITH BRIAN BOUCHER. WE WERE TALKing about life and hockey and everything we had been through. Partway through the night, Boucher looked at me said, "B, I don't know many other stories where two American kids grew up together and got drafted in the same round in the NHL."

"You know how we did it, don't you?" I said to Brian.

"No," he said, looking confused.

"Woonsocket," I said with a grin.

Growing up in a working-class family in a town like Woonsocket was the best thing that ever happened to me. Without Woonsocket, I never would have developed the skills to make it to the ice. And without my family, I never would have learned the lessons that held me together off of it.

In late 2018, my mom was diagnosed with colon cancer. Her family had a history of cancer, and she'd lost four siblings to the disease. We refused to lose another family member to it, and everyone in the family immediately stepped up. Mom was there for all of us growing up. No matter what it took and no matter who it was, Mom was there for us every single time we needed her. When I was at my lowest, trying to patch my body back together and relearn how to see, my mom had been there to take care of me every step of the way. Now it was our turn to take care of her.

From everything we have been told, Mom is going to win her battle with colon cancer. And the ordeal has reminded us just how close we are as a family, and how we can get through anything as long as we're together.

Today my injury is like any other player's old wound. I'm reminded of it every day, but I no longer think of it as an injury—it's just a fact of my life. It's amazing how quickly you can get used to a new normal. Before I got hurt, I had very sensitive eyes. I hated using eye drops of any kind when I was sick. Now I put eye drops in my right eye every day. Whenever it is cold out or I am feeling run-down, my right eye hurts. On those days, whenever I blink, it hurts, and I think to myself, "How did I play in the NHL with vision like this?"

I don't play hockey too much anymore. When I do, I don't skate as fast as I used to, and my body gets tired and sore more quickly. I can feel my back tighten if I twist too far or if I bump one of my problematic discs.

And yet, I still get a thrill every time I hit the ice. Every time I put on my skates, I go back to being a kid again. Suddenly I'm not looking through one eye at the arena rink in front of me—I'm riding my bike to the park, where the frozen pond is coming into view, the empty sheet of ice full of promise. Life might take me a lot of places, but I always come home.

Critics said I would never play in the NHL with one good eye, and I did. They said I would never come back from two back surgeries, and I did. Throughout my life, everything I have been told that I couldn't do, I went out and did anyway.

I found a way; I always found a way. " 'Never' does not exist," as my mom said.

You can knock me down, but I am going to keep getting up. And I'm never going to stop.

ACKNOWLEDGMENTS

FIRST AND FOREMOST, I WOULD LIKE TO THANK MY FAMILY FOR EVERYTHING they've done for me throughout my life.

Thanks to Lise and Norm Boucher.

Thanks to Bill Belisle, David Belisle, and Mount Saint Charles Academy.

Thank you to Jim Rutherford, Paul Maurice, and Pete DeBoer for letting me play for such a great organization in Junior.

Thanks to my agents, Tom Laidlaw and Paul Theofanous.

Thanks to my lawyers Mark Smith, Tom Harvey, and Howard Silber.

Thank you to Mike Milbury for trading for me, and then for trading me to the Leafs.

I'd like to thank Pat Quinn, Ken Dryden, and the Toronto Maple Leafs organization.

I am incredibly grateful to all of the doctors in Ottawa who operated on me and saved my eye. Thanks, too, to Chris Broadhurst and then Brent Smith, who stayed with me the night of my injury in Ottawa. And thank you to Dr. Stanley Chang for all of the surgeries that he performed, which allowed me to play hockey again.

ACKNOWLEDGMENTS

I'd like to thank Don Maloney, Glen Sather, and the New York Rangers for taking a chance on me after my injury.

I'd like to thank all my teammates and trainers with the Islanders, Leafs, Rangers, Bruins, Blackhawks, and Blue Jackets.

I'd like to thank the Woonsocket North Stars youth hockey organization and coaches, where it all began!

I'd like to thank Tie Domi for introducing me to Kevin Hanson and Brendan May at Simon & Schuster. Thanks to them both.

Thank you to Jim Lang for all the help on this project.

Finally, I would like to thank the fans for all their support.

—Bryan Berard

•   •   •

IN DECEMBER 2018, MY TRUSTY AGENT, BRIAN WOOD, CALLED ME WITH AN OFFER. Brian wanted to know if I would be interested in writing a book with Bryan Berard.

Of course, I had heard of Bryan Berard, and I knew all about his career and his devastating eye injury. But it wasn't until I started working with him on a regular basis that I really got to know what he was all about. And, like anyone else who has spent time with Bryan, I quickly came to like and respect the man.

As always, there are many people who made the writing of this book possible.

I would like to thank my wife, Patricia, and our daughters, Adriana and Cassandra. If it weren't for their patience and understanding, I would never have been able to finish the book on time.

ACKNOWLEDGMENTS

I would like to thank my mom and dad for giving me the gift of a sound work ethic.

Thanks again to Brian Wood for always having my back and always getting the deal done. (ABC: Always Be Closing).

The men and women at Simon & Schuster Canada are as good as it gets, and it all starts with the leadership of publisher Kevin Hanson.

Thanks again to senior editor Brendan May. As he has been on every book we have worked on, Brendan was the glue that held this project together.

Thanks to the management and staff at my radio station, 105.9 The Region, for being so accommodating during the writing process.

Several websites were crucial to telling Bryan's story. They include: NHL.com, TSN.ca, TheStar.com, postmedia.com, theglobeandmail.com, NYPost.com, NYDailynews.com, NHL.Com/Islanders, NHL.Com/MapleLeafs, NHL.Com/Blackhawks, Sportsnet.ca, Woonsocket-call.com, providencejournal.com, USAHockey.com, thehockeynews.com, ontariohockeyleague.com, Hockeydb.com, Hockey-reference.com, KHL.Ru, and YouTube.com.

There was a long list of friends who couldn't wait to speak to me about Bryan. Special thanks to the following individuals: Steve Thomas, former Leafs trainer Brent Smith, Paul Maurice (thanks to the Winnipeg Jets for all of your help), Jamie Allison, Brian Leetch, Jason Strudwick (Struddy), Brian Boucher, Jeff O'Neill, Mike Milbury, Tom Laidlaw, FBI special agent Matt Galioto, attorney Tom Harvey, Dave Belisle from the Mount Saint Charles hockey program, John Kaiser, and finally, Tyson Reed from Whale Rock Point Partners.

Bryan often spoke about how close he is with his family. After working with him on this book, I believe every single word of it. Thanks to his mom, Pam (don't ever mess with Pam), his brother Greg, and the rest of his brothers and sisters. Pam had an invaluable treasure trove of photos, clippings, and articles on Bryan, from the time he was first learning how to skate until the present day.

Finally, I would really like to thank Bryan.

With Bryan Berard, what you see is what you get. There is a not an ounce of BS in that man. If he has something to say, he is going to say it. His willingness to be so open and honest about everything that happened in his life—good, bad, and ugly—was impressive. Considering everything Bryan has gone through, you would think that he has some bitterness about him. In fact, the complete opposite is true.

Between January and May 2019, Bryan and I spoke at length at least once a week, sometimes more. I found him to be self-deprecating, humble, funny, brutally honest, and just a good guy. It is easy to see why all his friends, family, guys that he used to play with, and anyone else that took time to speak with me all said the same thing: Bryan was a great teammate, and he is still a great friend to this day.

Bryan Berard is the kind of person you want on your team, and I am lucky to have him on my team now.

Long live the Woonsocket Rocket!

—Jim Lang